The translingual imagination

THE TRANSLINGUAL IMAGINATION

Steven G. Kellman

University of Nebraska Press

Lincoln and London

© 2000 by the University of Nebraska Press
All rights reserved
Manufactured in the United States of America
∞
Library of Congress Cataloging-in-Publication Data
Kellman, Steven G., 1947–
The translingual imagination / Steven G. Kellman.
p. cm.
Includes bibliographical references (p.   ) and index.
ISBN 0-8032-2745-0 (cloth : alk. paper)
1. Multilingualism and literature.   2. Language and culture.
I. Title.
PN171.M93K45   2000
809—dc21   99-43624
CIP

CONTENTS

Preface   vii

1 Translingualism and the Literary Imagination   1
2 Pourquoi Translingual?   17
3 Translingual Africa   36
4 Coetzee Reads Beckett   50
5 Nabokov and the Psychomorphology of Zemblan   63
6 Eva Hoffman Lost in the Promised Land   73
7 Begley Joins the Firm   85
8 Sayles Goes Spanish   102

Epilogue   113

A Roster of Translingual Authors   117

Works Cited   119

Index   127

PREFACE

What song did the Sirens sing? Homer never tells us, perhaps because they did not sing in Greek. Not the least barbaric fact about the anthropophagous race of Cyclops is that they probably spoke an alien tongue. Wily Odysseus, who managed to cajole reluctant Philoctetes into joining the bloody battle at Troy, must have been adept at languages. In order to talk his way—sans dictionary or dragoman—past Circe, Calypso, the Phaiakians, the Lotus Eaters, and the Lastrygonians, this wandering king of Ithaca, this master of all ways of contending, surely must have had to pick up some of the native lingo of the places to which he traveled. Yet as far as Homer is concerned, the Mediterranean is a monolingual sink. It is all Greek to him.

Not every author has been as blind to the variety of human languages, however. Before he lost his sight, it is said, John Milton had read every book in every language that was then available in Europe, early in the age of printing. We do know that he wrote capably not merely in English but in Latin, Greek, and Hebrew, too. Yet the Babel myth, in one version or another, is among the oldest stories told in many cultures. According to Choctaw legend, everyone on Earth spoke Choctaw until arrogant humans tried to construct a mound that would touch the heavens. And once upon a time, before haughty authors climbed up ivory towers, the job of a translator was as incomprehensible as that of editor or literary agent. There probably never was an Ur-language, a perfect primal tongue that sufficed for the entire human race. But nostalgia for it, along with the moot premise that international conflict would vanish if only we all shared a common lexicon, accounts for the invention of Esperanto, Volapük, Ido, Langu Universelle, Bopal, Spelin, Dil, Balta, Veltparl, and other artificial languages. Like sex, language seems to be a bizarre stratagem by which human beings both connect and conflict.

Most inhabitants of this planet are at least bilingual. Yet particularly in the United States, a nation created in the shadow of Babel, many yearn to be done with other tongues. In revulsion against British oppression, revolutionary leaders debated adopting German (spoken by about 40 percent of colonial Pennsylvania), French, Latin, or Hebrew—anything but the language of the defeated tyrant—as the official language of their new republic. Benjamin Franklin, who studied more than a dozen languages and was agile enough in French to translate the American Constitution into it, began his career by publishing a newspaper in German. The United States was a tumultuous linguistic mix, until World War I led to prohibition of instruction and even conversation in German and other languages, and restrictive immigration laws in 1924 radically reduced the fresh supply of xenophones. Now in its third century, the United States is a place where the children of immigrants deny their mothers' tongues and many clamor for a single language, English. "If English was good enough for Jesus Christ, it's good enough for me" was the argument adduced by an American college student for exemption from an already feeble foreign language requirement.

English is good enough for King James, William Shakespeare, Jane Austen, Walt Whitman, Casey Stengel, Derek Walcott, and Howard Stern. English facilitates a vast array of thoughts and emotions, but as any other language does, it also limits these human expressions to what is possible within its repertoire of sounds and structures. Perhaps even more than ethnicity, language is a useful way of beginning to approach questions of identity, individual and collective. And the first thing to say, in any language, is that multilingualism enlarges. "Be all that you can be," urges the ad for the United States Army, and its language-training school fulfills the promise. If identity is shaped by language, then monolingualism is a deficiency disorder. It limits our versions of self, society, and universe. "Since the spirit which constantly reveals itself in the world can never be exhaustively known through any given number of views or opinions," argued Wilhelm von Humboldt, a polyglot who wrote in French and German, "it would be far better to multiply the languages on earth as many times as the number of earth's inhabitants might permit" (483).

This book examines literary translingualism, the phenomenon of authors who write in more than one language or at least in a language other than their primary one. The most celebrated literary translinguals of the twentieth century are Samuel Beckett, Joseph Conrad, and Vladimir Nabokov, but as the partial roster at the end of the volume suggests, thousands of writers, from antiquity to the present, have been translingual. They are among the most fascinating of literary figures because their lives took noticeably dramatic twists and because their position between languages enabled them to challenge the limits of their own literary medium. Moreover, translingualism is more than a categorical contrivance, a classification concocted to serve the purposes of idle pedantry. It is a genuine and rich tradition, one in which authors are acutely aware of shared conditions and aspirations. Chinua Achebe responds, explicitly and implicitly, to Conrad, Eva Hoffman to Mary Antin. Both J. M. Coetzee and Raymond Federman have written extensively about Beckett. Even when Nabokov is belittling "Conrad's souvenir-shop style, bottled ships and shell necklaces of romanticist clichés" (*Strong Opinions* 42), he is acknowledging affinity with another Anglophonic author who left behind a Slavic land and language.

"No instance exists of a person's writing two languages perfectly" (839), wrote Thomas Jefferson, in English, from Paris. But the author of the blotted Declaration of Independence probably would be hard put to cite the instance of a person's writing even *one* language perfectly. Perfection is not an attribute of postlapsarian, post-Babelian expression. Yet it is remarkable how compelling so many writers are able to be in a second, third, or even fourth language. And how persistent an antitranslingual animus has been, as if abandonment of the mother tongue—*Muttersprache, langue maternelle, mama loshen, sfat em, lengua materna, modersml, lingua materna, matesk jazyk*—were tantamount to matricide.

More than anyone else, William Butler Yeats was responsible for the reverent reception that Western readers accorded Rabindranath Tagore and for the fact that he was awarded the Nobel Prize for Literature in 1913. But Yeats later turned against "Damn

Tagore," berating the Bengali poet for daring to translate his own work into English. "Tagore does not know English, no Indian knows English," Yeats wrote in 1935. It was rather incongruous for an Irish nationalist to pose as the guardian of English purity, but while Yeats's compatriots were struggling to revive Gaelic as a language of literary expression, he was insisting that translingualism is impossible: "Nobody can write with music and style in a language not learned in childhood and ever since the language of his thought" (834).

Beckett's French came after childhood, in Dublin classrooms, and his *Molloy*, *Malone meurt*, and *L'Innommable* refute Yeats's thought. "I don't think that one can be a bilingual poet," T. S. Eliot contended: "I don't know of any case in which a man wrote great poetry or even fine poems equally well in two languages. I think one language must be the one you express yourself in in poetry, and you've got to give up the other for that purpose" (99). Eliot's dismissal of the subject is a bit too peremptory. He himself wrote a few indifferent poems in French, but the burden of this book is to examine the possibilities of writing equally well in two languages, or at least of writing well in an adopted language.

It is a truism that poems travel where poets cannot. Even if only in samizdat, tamizdat, and translation, texts take life despite the boundaries of nation and language. The recovery of antique texts in Greek animated the Renaissance in western Europe, and writings in Hebrew, Greek, and Arabic—the Hebrew Bible, the New Testament, and the Qur'an—transformed the world. Translingualism is a striking instance of invasive literary commerce within a single author. By defying linguistic borders, it implicitly recognizes them, reversing the romantic attempt to collapse all discourse into the colloquial. Authors who carefully construct their phrases in words that are not the common currency are rejecting Wordsworth's insistence that poets employ "the very language of men." Like the French *passé simple*, the special past tense employed exclusively in literary discourse, or like the archaic terms in English such as *forsooth*, *whilom*, and *alack*, translingualism verily enables writers and readers to go beyond the familiar words of the tribe. But it also embodies the romantic impulse toward cosmic expression. Panlingualism is the logical—and impossible—culmination of the urge to expand through yet another language.

Translingual transactions have occurred frequently throughout literary history, and they are wonderfully instructive to anyone interested in literature, language, and the connections between the two. Yet, though studies of individual translingual authors and of bilingualism in society abound, it is astonishing that almost nothing has been written about the general phenomenon of literary translingualism. Useful exceptions include Leonard Forster's *The Poet's Tongues*, Jane Miller's essay "Writing in a Second Language," and Elizabeth Klosty Beaujour's *Alien Tongues*. Under the direction of Marc Shell and Werner Sollors, the Longfellow Institute of Harvard University has dedicated itself to the long-term project of recovering and studying the literature of the United States written in languages other than English, and the forthcoming volumes of the *Longfellow Anthology of American Literature*, published by New York University Press, will make available the texts of many stubbornly monolingual authors who insisted on clinging to Arabic, French, German, Greek, Navajo, Norwegian, Ojibwa, Russian, Turkish, Welsh, or Yiddish rather than accede to the ambient English. It will also include translinguals, such as Luigi Ventura, whose winsome novella *Peppino*, about fellow Italian immigrants in New York, was apparently written in French(!), and Jeannette Lander, who, though born in New York and reared in Atlanta, moved to Berlin in the 1960s and writes her novels, set in the American South, in German laced with Yiddish and African-American dialogue. In the new *Multilingual America*, Sollors collects essays on American literature that is written in languages other than English. The Recovery project of Arte Público Press in Houston has been concentrating on publishing neglected texts of Latino authors, many in Spanish and many written by translinguals. However, much still remains to be learned about other languages, other groups, and other countries beyond the United States.

I am very grateful for a semester at the Longfellow Institute, where, as a John E. Sawyer Fellow, I was able to hone my own ideas on translingualism in the brilliant company of Shell, Sollors, and the polyglot faculty and students assembled for their seminars. An NEH Summer Seminar at the University of Natal at Pietermaritzburg, in the Republic of South Africa, enabled me to reduce some of my vast ignorance about African literatures, and I thank its directors, Bernth Lindfors and David Attwell, and fellow seminarians for their expert assistance and generous forbearance while I hunted translingualism throughout that huge continent. Students in several courses at the University of Texas at San Antonio have suffered through and contributed to my developing ideas about the subject. A UTSA Faculty Research Leave and a UTSA Faculty Research Grant assisted me in the completion of this book.

The editors of *Comparative Literature Studies*, *Criticism*, the *Hollins Critic*, *Hopscotch*, and *Prooftexts* provided encouragement and publication for stages of my ideas about translingualism. Parts of chapter 4, "Coetzee Reads Beckett," were published as "J. M. Coetzee and Samuel Beckett: The Translingual Link" in *Comparative Literature Studies* 33.2 (1996): 161–72 (copyright 1996, Pennsylvania State University; reproduced by permission of The Pennsylvania State University Press). Parts of chapter 1, "Translingualism and the Literary Imagination," appeared under the same title in *Criticism* 33.4 (1991): 527–41. Parts of chapter 7, "Begley Joins the Firm," were published as "Louis Begley Joins the Firm" in *Hollins Critic* 36.3 (1999): 1-11. Parts of chapter 8, "Sayles Goes Spanish," appeared under the same title in *Hopscotch* 1 (1999). Parts of chapter 6, "Eva Hoffman in the Promised Land," were published as "Lost in the Promised Land: Eva Hoffman Revises Mary Antin" in *Prooftexts* 18 (1998): 149–59 (© 1998, Johns Hopkins University Press).

Through his example and his wise and sympathetic readings, Ilan Stavans has helped me understand what I am trying to describe. My language is inadequate to express my gratitude to Wendy Barker. I am indebted to the staff at the University of Nebraska Press for their enthusiastic support.

Books conclude, but our reading of languages and literatures cannot. The complete guide to the translingual imagination would feature separate chapters on Fernando Pessoa, Petrarch, Prem Chand, Yehuda Halevi, and dozens of other prodigies. The ideal student of translingualism would be a polyglot polymath, a monster of erudition who would know far more than I about Chinese who compose poetry in Korean, or Finns who render fiction in Swedish. If translingualism advances to its limits in the utopia of panlingualism, a scholar can merely long for omniscience and bite his tongue. With this modest part of the story of translingualism, I stop here, waiting for you.

THE TRANSLINGUAL IMAGINATION

1
TRANSLINGUALISM AND THE LITERARY IMAGINATION

Though he was the most illustrious of all basketball guards, Michael Jordan failed spectacularly when he attempted a career in professional baseball. Like a language, each sport entails a distinctive aptitude, history, protocol, and weltanschauung. There is no reason to suppose that a star in one sport will necessarily excel in another, any more than that Demosthenes would have become a consummate orator in Malinke, Gujarati, or Ojibwa as well as Greek. William Blake and Michelangelo each produced important paintings and poems, but few other major creators have distinguished themselves in more than one art form. Paul Bowles wrote fiction and music. Henri Michaux was a poet and a painter. Yukio Mishima and Ousmane Sembene have each expressed themselves through both novel and film. And Jean Cocteau produced novels, plays, films, ballets, and drawings. But such transdisciplinary fluency is rare, and even more rare is the instance in which the same person does more than dabble in a second medium. The history of sculpture was not transformed by anyone who also transformed the history of music.

For an explanation, we might need look no further than the law of the conservation of cultural energy. Each art form makes sufficient demands of its own to monopolize the talents and energies of anyone. In the throes of composing *King Lear*, Shakespeare had no compulsion to express himself symphonically, even if he had had the temperament, the talent, and the orchestra. In post-Renaissance capitalist culture, industrial specialization has reduced the *uomo universale*—and his female counterpart—to a mere dilettante.

The same might be said of the polyglot, in whatever language it is said. A majority of the world's population is at least *bi*lingual. Fortunately, few speakers are writers. Fewer still write well. And rarer still are those who write well in a second language. It is demanding enough to put the right words in the right place in one's native tongue. "All you do," noted sportswriter Red Smith, "is sit down at a typewriter and open a vein" (Hendrickson 208). How vain, then, are those who presume to write imaginative literature in a foreign tongue. "No man fully capable of his own language ever masters another" proclaimed George Bernard Shaw (733)—who, despite the multilingual accomplishments of Isak Dinesen, Buchi Emecheta, Lea Goldberg, Joyce Mansour, Bharati Mukherjee, Elsa Triolet, and others, would probably have extended the pronouncement to women as well. The poet Marina Tsvetaeva wrote in three languages: Russian, French, and German. And in a letter that she composed in German to Rainer Maria Rilke, who himself excelled in both German and French, she remarked that Goethe (in his notes to *West-Östlicher Divan*) insisted that no one can ever achieve anything of significance in a foreign language (Rilke, 6 July 1926).

Though raised in Spanish, George Santayana wrote his poetry in English. Yet he declared that no poets can be great who do not use the language in which their mothers sang them lullabies. For that reason, he slighted his own verse:

> Of impassioned tenderness or Dionysiac frenzy I have nothing, nor even of that magic and pregnancy of phrase—really the creation of a fresh idiom—which marks the high lights of poetry. Even if my temperament had been naturally warmer, the fact that the English language (and I can write no other with assurance) was not my mother-tongue would of itself preclude any inspired use of it on my part; its roots do not quite reach to my center. I never drank in in childhood the homely cadences and ditties which in pure spontaneous poetry set the essential key. I know no words redolent of the wonder-world, fairy-tale, or the cradle. (vii–viii)

Vladimir Nabokov described his own switch from brilliant Russian to bravura English as "exceedingly painful—like learning anew to handle things after losing seven or eight fingers in an explosion" (*Strong Opinions* 54).

There seems something not only painful but unnatural, almost matricidal, about an author who abandons the *Muttersprache*, and it is instructive that the most universally venerated of all authors, William Shakespeare, never left England or English. By twentieth-century standards, erudite Ben Jonson's assessment of Shakespeare's "small Latin and less Greek" is severe, but it does point to the premise—built into John Milton's description in "L'Allegro" of the Bard's warbling his native wood-notes wild—that his greatness is more a matter of nature than art. If Shakespeare had not remained faithful to his first language, Schiller might have hesitated over classifying him *naiv* rather than *sentimentalisch*. In the one extended use of a foreign language in a Shakespeare play, *Henry V*, English triumphs when Katherine catalogues parts of the body and trades in French terms for their English counterparts. "Only in the mother tongue can one speak one's own truth," declared Paul Celan in German, a language he came to after Romanian, French, and Russian. Yet German was indeed his mother tongue, the tongue in which his beloved mother read to him (see Chalfen) and the language in which he composed his searing poetry. For Elias Canetti, who grew up in a quadralingual household, German was also "a belated mother tongue" (*Memoirs* 76), the language that his beloved mother drilled into him, at the age of eight, after Ladino, Bulgarian, and English. Acquired from his *Mutter* in Francophonic Lausanne, German was the language on which Canetti would base his literary career and his life: "I was reborn under my mother's influence to the German language, and the spasm of that birth produced the passion tying me to both, the language and my mother. Without these two, basically one and the same, the further course of my life would have been senseless and incomprehensible" (*Memoirs* 80).

When linguistic maternity is multiple, it is difficult to determine precisely which is the mother tongue. Vladimir Nabokov and George Steiner both claim to have been reared equally in three tongues. In the households of the educated elite in Africa and India, children often learn a European language simultaneously with an indigenous one, and though each has a distinct function, neither holds primacy, in chronology or in fluency, over the other. Salman Rushdie has declared Urdu to be his first language, but he has done all his professional writing in English, a language he also spoke from early childhood and grew to be more at home with through living abroad. Because languages are incessantly evolving within communities, John Barth and Thomas Pynchon had to acquire proficiency in what is virtually a foreign tongue—eighteenth-century English—in order to write, respectively, *The Sot-Weed Factor* and *Mason and Dixon*. Likewise, neither language nor the relationship between languages is ever static for an individual speaker. In a sense, every speaker is translingual, moving with if not through languages.

Eva Hoffman lived in Polish for her first thirteen years, but when she revisits Cracow in middle age, she describes herself as struggling to find the right local words. Gerda Lerner fled Vienna at the age of eighteen, and half a century later, when she returns to lecture, in labored German, on a book she had written in English, she warns her audience: "You may wonder at my peculiar accent, and often at my choice of words. Although I am a native German speaker, I have not really spoken German in fifty years, and I have never before lectured in German" (47). Though German was Lerner's mother tongue, it had long since ceased to be her primary one. When, fifty years after quitting St. Petersburg, Nabokov, whose books had been available to native speakers only in samizdat, translated *Lolita* into Russian, it was in a quaint, archaic idiom foreign to them and the author. Yet a 1999 poll among readers of the newspaper *Moskovskii Komsomoletz* ranked *Lolita*, a great English novel, number twelve among great Russian novels of the twentieth century.

James Clifford insists that anthropology alter its paradigm from that of an outside expert who intervenes within a stable, homogeneous community. Just as Clifford's "traveling cultures" (17–46), in which both observer and observed are hybrid and fluid, with language, too, speakers and speech communities are forever in flux, and it becomes futile to try to establish priorities. According to Herodotus, the Egyptian monarch Psamtik tried to determine which was the primordial language of our species by ordering that two infants be raised in absolute linguistic isolation. When the first syllables they uttered, without benefit of imitation, sounded like *bekos*, the Phrygian word for bread, the pharaoh concluded that Phrygian is the mother tongue of the human race. By defying linguistic boundaries, translingualism mocks a mockery of such specious attempts at hierarchy.

What gives George Frideric Handel a credible claim to the title of greatest English composer is the fact that, despite his thick German accent, the music he composed in London eclipses that of Henry Purcell, Edward Elgar, and Benjamin Britten. Tardiness in acquiring American English did not prevent Albert Bierstadt, Willem de Kooning, Arshile Gorky, Hans Hofmann, Mark Rothko, Ben Shahn, Joseph Stella, and Max Weber from attaining prominent positions in American painting. However, poetry is not nearly as portable. Much more than music, painting, sculpture, or dance, language is anchored to the complexities of a particular time and place. "He who wants to dedicate himself to painting should start by cutting out his tongue" is the sentence with which Henri Matisse starts his book *Jazz* and the concept with which he distinguishes his wordless, nomadic art from that of poets.

If Handel had been an author rather than a composer, he would have had to confront two options after choosing exile: either continue to compose in German, in stubborn isolation from the environment in which he lived, or else switch to English, though it is very difficult for an adult to attain the fluency and even mastery in a second language that is necessary for literary virtuosity. After escaping Nazi Europe in her adolescence, Gerda Lerner aspired to be a writer but found herself caught between the native German that she sought to discard and the American English that tormented her: "Living in translation is like skating on wobbly skates over thin ice. There is no sure footing; there are no clear-cut markers; no obvious signposts. It helps to trust in one's balance, to swing free and make leaps of the imagination. I suppose what I am saying is that it is immensely strenuous. Quite apart from being alienating" (40). For those who live in and through words, living in translation is to be racked between life and death.

W. H. Auden continued to create important poetry after leaving his native land, but he merely traded one Anglophonic country (England) for another (the United States). "Due to the Curse of Babel," proclaimed Auden in 1962, "poetry is the most provincial of the arts." However, he saw grandeur in that affliction, the fact that an art that depends on language thwarts its own potential for relocation. To sabotage a sonnet by robbing it of mobility, either deprive it of its feet or compose it in Uzbek—or any other finite language. "Today, when civilization is becoming monotonously the same all the world over," Auden declared, "one feels inclined to regard this [poetry's provincialism] as a blessing rather than a curse; in poetry, at least, there cannot be an 'International Style' " (23). For Vincent Van Gogh, living in Arles instead of Amsterdam would have been more of a handicap and less of an inspiration had he tried to use words rather than pigments to portray starry nights.

And yet modernism is largely a literature of exile, a project of psychic, if not geographical, dislocation. Almost two millennia after Ovid suffered the adversity of making Latin verse in Tomi, some of modernism's most influential champions have stubbornly clung to their native languages thousands of miles from where it is spoken. Consider Gertrude Stein parsing her perverse English in Paris, Witold Gombrowicz and Czesław Miłosz composing in their Polish in Buenos Aires and Berkeley, respectively, Isaac Bashevis Singer persisting with Yiddish and José Martí with Spanish in New York, Marguérite Yourcenar spinning fine French on Mount Desert Island, Thomas Mann conjuring up a German *Doktor Faustus* in Santa Monica, and Alexander Solzhenitsyn pronouncing in Russian from the fastness of rural Vermont. O. E. Rölvaag did not abandon his native Norwegian when he settled in Minnesota and wrote *I de dage* (1924) and *Riket grundlæges* (1925), which, translated as *Giants in the Earth* in 1928, entered the canon of American literature. Nor did Federico García Lorca resort to the ambient English to compose *Poeta en Nueva York* when he was a poet in New York in 1929. Ernest Hemingway and Julio Cortázar in Paris, Paul Bowles in Tangier, Nelly Sachs and Peter Weiss in Sweden, Ezra Pound in Italy, Robert Graves in Majorca, Malcolm Lowry in Mexico, James Joyce in Trieste, Zurich, and Paris—all are heroic figures of the artist who maintains literary loyalty to the native language far from the native land. Stephan G. Stephansson, considered the major Icelandic poet of the twentieth century, lives in Canada. Lars Gustafsson writes novels in his native Swedish while residing in Austin, Texas, and Turkish poet Seyfettin Basçillar is chief meat inspector for northern New Jersey.

However, this century also offers abundant examples of the converse: authors who, sometimes even without relocating, have excelled in a second, third, or even fourth language. George Steiner, himself equally fluent in English, French, and German, has pondered the "extraterritoriality" of much twentieth-century literature—how poets have become "unhoused and wanderers across languages" (*Extraterritorial* 11). S. Y. Agnon, Samuel Beckett, Joseph Conrad, Kateb Yacine, Clarice Lispector, Nathalie Sarraute, Tom Stoppard, and Wole Soyinka, among many others, developed important voices in languages that are not those in which their mothers sang them lullabies. Elie Wiesel, who writes in French (his fifth language, after Yiddish, Hebrew, Hungarian, and German) but resides in the United States, and Elias Canetti, whose first language was Ladino but who wrote in German though he lived in London, combine the linguistic agility of a Nabokov with the geographical itinerancy of Marco Polo, who himself chose French not Italian to recount his travels to China. Colonialism, war, increased mobility, and the aesthetics of alienation have combined to create a canon of translingual literature. It seems no mere coincidence that leading figures in the Theater of the Absurd, drama that foregrounds language and subverts communication, were translingual or from multilingual backgrounds—Samuel Beckett, Arthur Adamov, Fernando Arrabal, Eugène Ionesco, and Michel de Ghelderode.

The most ostentatious and willful case of translingualism is the small body of fiction and poetry created in Esperanto, the vernacular of no one, an artificial language barely a century old. And the oddest contribution of American Esperantists is the screenplay *Incubus* (1965), which, directed by Leslie Stevens and starring William Shatner and Milos Milos, became the only feature film ever made in that fabricated language. But the phenomenon of translingualism antedates the modern aspiration to purify the words of the tribe by substituting the words of another tribe. Spanish-American literature commences with Garcilaso de la Vega, who wrote his masterpiece, *Comentarios reals*, in Spanish rather than his native Quechua. Latin literature—which is said to have begun with Livius Andronicus, a Greek slave who wrote a Latin version of the *Odyssey*—was in no small measure the creation of men who adopted the language of Rome even though they were from Spain (like Seneca, Quintilian, Martial, and Lucan), or from Gaul (like Ausonius), or from Africa (like Apuleius, Terence, and Augustine). Later, Renaissance men demonstrated their versatility through languages as well as disciplines; Erasmus in Holland, More in England, and Descartes in France were acting as translinguals when they neglected their local dialects to write major texts in what was the adoptive language of the European intellectual empire—the language in which, though he was proficient in Spanish, Dutch, and Hebrew, Baruch Spinoza composed his *Ethica*. Arabic, Mandarin, Persian, Russian, and Sanskrit have also served as linguae francae, the dominant second language of heterogeneous speech communities. The emergence of written literature in sub-Saharan Africa cannot be understood apart from the role of English, French, and Portuguese as translingual media.

Apuleius begins *The Golden Ass* by recounting how he studied Greek and then, "Mox in urbe Latia advena studiorum, Quiritium indigenam sermonem aerumnabili labore, nullo magistro praeeunte, aggressus excolui" (2) [Soon after (as a stranger) I arrived at Rome, where by great industry, and without instruction of any schoolmaster, I arrived at the full perfection of the Latin tongue" (3)]. It is precisely the luxuriance—the prodigious vocabulary and ornate syntax—of Apuleius's Latin, like Nabokov's English, that makes the original text of *The Golden Ass* such a challenge to the modern reader. As a linguistic interloper, Apuleius has much more to prove than native masters like Virgil or Horace, and he pleads forgiveness—elegantly, disingenuously—for any crudeness in his use of Latin: "En ecce praefamur veniam, si quid exotici ac forensis sermonis rudis locutor offendero" (2) [I first crave and beg your pardon, lest I should happen to displease or offend any of you by the rude and rustic utterance of this strange and foreign language (3)]. However, before beginning his elaborate account of Lucius's many metamorphoses, Apuleius also notes that translingualism is particularly apt for a story about transformations such as his is—a tale in which the boundaries between species are porous: "Iam haec equidem ipsa vocis immutatio desultoriae scientiae stilo quem accessimus respondet" (4) [And verily this change of speech doth correspond to the enterprise and matter whereof I purpose to treat, like a rider leaping from horse to horse

(3, 5)]. As Franz Kafka, the Jew writing in Prague in German, also demonstrates, metamorphosis is a pertinent theme for translingual authors.

Not the least dramatic of the transformations in European culture during the millennium following the fall of Rome was the displacement of Latin by the local vernaculars. It was not a facile process, and the anxiety of translingualism is registered in the passionate apologias written by polyglot champions of languages other than Latin, all of whom enjoyed the luxury of linguistic choice. In *De vulgari eloquentia* Dante makes a lucid case—in Latin!—for the Florentine dialect as the best medium for poetry. John Wyclif, who preached in Latin and in English, was condemned as a heretic for encouraging translation of the Bible and the use of English for the benefit of monolingual parishioners. "Secler lordys schuld, in defawte of prelatys, lerne and preche þe law of God in here modyr tonge" (114), he chose to declare in his native tongue. Yet as late as 1545, Roger Ascham was using English to disparage the use of English: "And as for ye Latin or greke tonge, euery thyng is so excellently done in them, that none can do better: In the Englysh tonge contrary, euery thinge in a maner so meanly, bothe for the matter and handelynge that no man can do worse" (xiv). Such critical detachment from the very medium of criticism is possible only for a translingual, a writer who resides between languages. The modern science of linguistics could not be practiced except by those conversant with more than one language. Ludwig Wittgenstein, the philosopher who did most in the twentieth century to focus attention on the constraints of language, inhabited the space between German and English.

According to Aulus Gellius, the Latin epic poet Ennius was torn among three languages—"Quintus Ennius tria corda habere sese dicebat, quod loqui Graece et Osce et Latine sciebat" (262) [Quintus Ennius used to say that he had three hearts, because he knew how to speak Greek, Oscan, and Latin (263)]. Two millennia later, George Steiner claims a similar trilingualism: "I have no recollection whatever of a first language. So far as I am aware, I possess equal currency in English, French, and German" (*After Babel* 115). Similarly William Gerhardi, a British subject born in St. Petersburg, claims in *Memoirs of a Polyglot*—which he wrote in English in 1931—to have had from childhood a comparable facility in Russian, French, and German. And, for all the pathos of his plight as a Russian writer forced to start over again in Germany, France, and the United States, Nabokov—who admits in his autobiography *Speak, Memory* that he read English before Russian—was from his (privileged) childhood almost equally fluent in Russian, English, and French. His translingual dexterity is only underscored by the elegance with which he berates—in English—his own command of English for lacking the resources of a mother tongue: "the baffling mirror, the black velvet backdrop, the implied associations and traditions—which the native illusionist, frac-tails flying, can magically use to transcend the heritage in his own way" ("On a Book Entitled *Lolita*" 319). Nabokov's claims of linguistic inadequacy, like those of Apuleius, are manifestly inaccurate.

Many translinguals are consummate technicians, all the more fastidious for the fact that they are conscious of working with unfamiliar materials. But some are simply clumsy in the alien idiom. Recounting in meticulous English prose the story of translingual transformation that became her first novel, *How the García Girls Lost Their Accents*, Julia Alvarez—a Dominican immigrant to the United States—demonstrates that she has lost her own accent as well. Yet some translingual texts expose the accents that their authors never quite discard. It does not require preternatural perspicacity to spot occasional calques in the writings of some of the most respected translinguals, instances in which the author is thinking in one language but employing the locutions of another. Someone who, when asked his age, replies "I have thirty-five years" might well be a Francophone who is thinking "J'ai trente-cinq ans" or a Spanish-speaker merely transposing the phrase "Tengo treinta y cinco años" word-for-word into English. When John F. Kennedy declared "Ich bin ein Berliner," he was translating verbatim from English, unaware that use of the indefinite article in this German context renders the meaning "I am a jelly doughnut."

József Teodor Konrad Korzeniowski managed to reinvent himself as Joseph Conrad, one of the major novelists of the century, in a language, English, that he came to only in his twenties, after Polish and French. To his dying day, Conrad spoke English with an accent so thick it was sometimes incomprehensible to his wife,

Jessie, nor did his written command of English entirely disguise the author's translingualism. In *The Secret Agent*, when Conrad states that Adolf Verloc "pulled up violently the venetian blind" (84) and that, gazing at Winnie Verloc, Ossipon "was excessively terrified at her" (254), the calques of word order and choice betray the traces of incomplete translingualism. In *The Joys of Motherhood*, when Buchi Emecheta tells us that Nnu Ego's daughters "never really had sufficient to eat" (203) and that the lawyer Nweze "intervened . . . timely" (216), the Anglophone reader can suppose that these are calques on the author's native Ibo.

Is it churlish to quibble over translingual solecisms? Joseph Brodsky was a major figure in Russian poetry—who nevertheless also managed to become poet laureate of the United States—but his ability to create a volume of poetry in English did not in itself impress John Bayley. Reviewing *So Forth: Poems* for the *New York Times Book Review*, the British critic complained: "There is an inherent clumsiness about this, like a bear playing the flute, that is embarrassing" (Bayley 6). Canine rather than ursine, the metaphor in Samuel Johnson's infamous quip about homiletic women is equally applicable to translingual efforts: "Sir," observed the lexicographer to James Boswell, "a woman's preaching is like a dog's walking on his hinder legs. It is not done well: but you are surprized to find it done at all" (*Life* 287). Though the mere existence of translingual literature is a marvel, some of the writing has been done surprisingly well, and a few misplaced adverbs or inappropriate prepositions do not negate the odd fascination of the phenomenon.

All else being equal, translingualism is a more arduous process for a poet or a short story writer, whose primary unit is the individual, irreducible word, than it is for the novelist or playwright, who can divert us from solecisms with compelling plots and characters and for whom language might be merely instrumental. It is difficult to imagine Stéphane Mallarmé writing in any language other than his inimitable, untranslatable French, though another poet, one less dependent on the evocative sonics and semiotics of particular syllables, might manage the transition. One can more easily picture Henry Wadsworth Longfellow—who was in fact an accomplished linguist and, as the first professor of comparative literature at Harvard, a champion of multilingualism—composing in German. When a storyteller stumbles over an idiom or two, you are still inclined to turn the page. The fact that Rafael Sabatini, who was born in Italy and schooled in Portugal and Switzerland, chose to write all his novels in his *sixth* language, English, did not diminish their popularity. Sabatini attributed his translingual choice to the fact that "all the best stories are written in English," and devoted readers of *Scaramouche*, *Captain Blood*, and *The Sea Hawk*, who do not pause for verbal nits, consider those among them. Flaubert stuck to French, but ten years after immigrating to the United States from Russia in 1926, Ayn Rand wrote her first novel, *We the Living*—as she did all her subsequent books—in English, and devoted disciples of objectivism do not cavil over language.

Beyond qualitative distinctions, some categorical ones are useful. A taxonomy of literary translingualism would begin by differentiating between authors who have written important works in more than one language, the *ambilinguals*, and those who have written in only a single language but one other than their native one, the *monolingual translinguals*. Petrarch is probably the most dexterous of several early Renaissance poets who distinguished themselves in Latin as well as the vernacular; he is a significant figure in both Latin and Italian literatures. If Nabokov had never left Europe and written his later stories and novels in English, he would still be counted a major author in Russian literature, as is Mendele Mokher Sforim in the history of both Yiddish and Hebrew. Prem Chand pioneered modern fiction in Urdu and then proceeded to do the same in Hindi. Mizra Asadullah Khan Ghalib, considered by many to be the greatest poet in Urdu, also excelled in Persian and is another ambilingual translingual.

So, too, are Chingiz Aitmatov (Kyrgyz and Russian), Vassilis Alexakis (Greek and French), Samuel Beckett (English and French), André Brink (Afrikaans and English), Rosalia de Castro (Galician and Castilian), Ernest Claes (Flemish and German), Rosario Ferré (Spanish and English), Mehmed bin Süleyman Fuzulî (Turkish, Persian, and Arabic), José-Maria de Heredia (Spanish and French), Vicente Huidobro (Spanish and French), Kaka Kalelkar (Hindi and Gujarati), Kateb Yacine (French and Arabic), Milan Kundera (Czech and French), Lin Yu-t'ang (Chinese and English), Muhammad Iqbal (Persian and Urdu), Francisco Manuel de Melo

(Portuguese and Spanish), Flann O'Brien (Irish and English), Okot p'Bitek (Aoli and English), Sa'di (Persian and Arabic), Sa'ib of Tabriz (Persian and Turkish), Antonio Tabucchi (Italian and Portuguese), Elsa Triolet (Russian and French), Gabre-Medhin Tsegaye (Amharic and English), and Giuseppe Ungaretti (Italian and French). In the seventeenth century, Narayanatirtha and Ksettraya each composed poetry in both Sanskrit and Telugu. Many of the Jewish poets of medieval Spain, including Abraham Ibn Ezra, Solomon Ibn Gabirol, and Yehuda Halevi, wrote in both Hebrew and Arabic. Julien Green, who was born in Paris to American parents, wrote most of his fiction in French, though he set much of it in the American South and could, and did, write an autobiography in English. Charles V proclaimed: "I speak German to my horses, Spanish to my God, French to my friends, and Italian to my mistresses." And as emperor of the Holy Roman Empire, he spoke with authority in each language. As agile as Proteus, ambilinguals promise the comprehensive, stereoscopic wisdom of Tiresias.

Kamala Das compartmentalizes her sensibilities between literary genres and assigns a different language to each: her native Malayalam to prose fiction and English to poetry. "I speak three languages, write in / Two, dream in one," writes Das in English in "An Introduction," a poem in which the Indian author concedes that English is not her native tongue but then asks: "Why not let me speak in / Any language I like?" As an ambilingual translingual, Das is able to raise pointed questions about the role of choice in the adoption of a particular literary medium. Is it possible to will oneself into becoming a great English novelist without having studied the language before adolescence? Does the writer choose the language, or does the language choose the writer? The most willful of ambilingual translinguals are those who choose to rework the "same" material in another language. If Melville had been able to recast *Moby-Dick* into Italian, he would have been reinventing the whale, functioning—as Baudelaire did when adapting his own poem as a *poème en prose* and as Beethoven did when scoring his violin concerto for piano—within an alternative system of articulation. A study of Abraham Cahan's *Yekl* in both Yiddish and English, of Vladimir Nabokov's *Lolita* in both English and Russian, and of Isak Dinesen's *Seven Gothic Tales* in both

English and Danish would reveal much about the creative process and about the expressive possibilities of different languages.

The case of monolingual translinguals suggests the limitations and illusions of linguistic freedom: even those able to step outside their native tongues are restricted in the further steps they take. Though ambilingual Yvan Goll made his choice between French and German again each time he wrote, Adelbert von Chamisso wrote all his poems in German rather than his native French. Born in Romania, Elie Wiesel was fluent in several languages when he was deported to Auschwitz. After the war, he studied another one, French, in Paris and made it the medium of all his fiction, even after he moved to the United States in 1956. Other monolingual translinguals who jumped a tongue and stuck with it include Conrad (Polish to English, via French), Elena Poniatowska (French to Spanish), Michael Arlen (Armenian to English), Fazil Iskander (Abkhaz to Russian), Tristan Tzara (Romanian to French), Wole Soyinka (Yoruba to English), Nikolai Gogol (Ukrainian to Russian), Kazuo Ishiguro (Japanese to English), Salman Rushdie (Urdu to English), Léopold Senghor (Wolof to French), Elias Canetti (Ladino to German), and Tom Stoppard (Czech to English).

The prodigious Isaac Asimov was born in Russia and reared in Yiddish, but he wrote all of his 477 books in English. Though Jeannette Lander sets her novels—*Ein Sommer in der Woche der itke K.* (1971), *Die Töchter* (1978), *Uberbleibsel* (1995)—in Atlanta, where she moved as a child from her native New York, she emigrated to Berlin in the 1960s and adopted German exclusively as her literary medium. Richard Rodriguez's memoir *Hunger of Memory* recounts his life as a trajectory from Spanish, the mother tongue he now barely remembers, to English, the language in which he has created a career as professional author. *Lost in Translation: A Life in a New Language* tells the story of how Ewa Wydra abandoned Poland and Polish to become Eva Hoffman, who writes her books only in American English. Other recent translingual memoirs that, written in fluent English, confirm that their author has abandoned the native tongue include Julia Alvarez's *Something to Declare* (Spanish to English) and Luc Sante's *The Factory of Facts* (French to English), both published in 1998. Though he published *Heading South, Looking North: A*

Bilingual Journey (1998) in English, Ariel Dorfman has declared his intention to produce a Spanish version as well. The dedication, to the author's wife, Angélica, celebrates Dorfman's own ambilingual translingualism: "It's my story, the story of my many exiles and my three countries and the two languages that raged for my throat during years and that now share me, the English and the Spanish that I have finally come to love almost as much as I love you."

Texts by translinguals usually reveal traces of their authors' other tongues, but most are written entirely in one language or another. Linguistic purity is of course a chimera; English, Korean, and Arabic are each already mongrel, and creolization among existing languages proceeds wherever cultures touch and collide—which is to say, virtually everywhere. Franglais, Spanglish, Germerican, Fanagalo, Gullah, Bajan, Papiamentu, Tok Pisin, Manipravalam, and other composites testify to how porous are the boundaries among languages. Code-switching is common among bilingual speakers, and authors who would represent speech as it is actually spoken create internally translingual texts, often between colloquial and formal or between regional and standard forms of the same language. Any writer of any scope is always ranging between registers. Toni Morrison, Ishmael Reed, and other African-American authors frequently switch between standard and Ebonic (black) English.

Code-switching is especially prominent among Mexican-American authors, who assert their hybrid identity by producing sentences that are neither entirely Spanish nor entirely English. Celebrating her own *mestizaje*, Gloria Anzaldúa, for one, announces "I am a border woman" and justifies the mingling of different registers of Spanish and English in *Borderlands / La Frontera* by explaining: "The switching of codes in this book from English to Castillian Spanish to the Northern Mexican dialect to Tex-Mex to a sprinkling of Nahuatl to a mixture of all of these, reflects my language, a new language—the language of the Borderlands" (preface).

In his *Klail City Death Trip* cycle of novels, a project that attempts to represent Chicano experience in the Rio Grande Valley throughout the twentieth century, Rolando Hinojosa-Smith writes his narrative of the early decades entirely in Spanish and the more recent ones entirely in English. To create plausible dialogue among his bilingual characters, however, Hinojosa-Smith often switches codes within the same sentence. For example, one of the letters that Jehú Malacara sends to Rafa Buenrostro in the epistolary novel *Mi querido Rafa* begins: "Lunch at the Camelot; Noddy me mandó (& *that's* the word, son) a que fuera a look over a deal; Noddy se quiere deshacer de la agencia de carros y el buyer wants (has) to use the bank's money for said purpose" (17). Though he might be exasperating to purists of Spanish and English, Hinojosa-Smith's purposes differ from those of Stefan George in contriving his own language out of fragments of Latin, Provençal, Catalan, and Spanish; the Klail City cycle simulates the code-switching actually employed by speakers in the south Texas context that Hinojosa-Smith evokes.

John Sayles has no personal ethnic connections to Spanish, but when he decided to write a novel about Cuban exiles in Miami, he chose *Los Gusanos* (The worms) as its title, appropriating the derogatory term that Fidel Castro applies to his opponents. And Sayles casts much of the dialogue in Spanish to simulate the speech that such characters would in fact employ. He made *Hombres armados*, his 1997 film about Central American guerrillas, almost entirely in Spanish.

Demographic verisimilitude dictates language choice in much realistic fiction. However, mirth rather than mimesis is the motive for mingling vernaculars with a debased form of Latin in medieval Goliardic drinking songs. But the linguistic amalgam that T. S. Eliot creates in *The Waste Land* and Ezra Pound in his *Cantos* is aimed at a synoptic vision that transcends the limitations of any particular language. A similar ambition is evident in the *plurilinguismo* of Italian novelist Sebastiano Vassalli's *Narcissus* (1968). Along with the ideal insomnia that it demands of readers, James Joyce's *Finnegans Wake* aspires to a consummate translingualism, a state beyond any of the many natural languages out of which the novel is compounded. Translinguals move beyond their native languages, but for many, particularly in the twentieth century, theirs is an aspiration to transcend language in general, to be pandictic, to utter everything. Impatient with the imperfections of finite verbal systems, they yearn to pass beyond words, to silence and truth.

2

POURQUOI TRANSLINGUAL?

Much translingual writing—like the growing body of work produced in German by newcomers from Turkey and other parts of the Levant that has been called *Gastarbeiterliteratur* (guest-worker literature)—is the literature of immigration. Though born in Turkey, Zehra Cirak lives in Berlin and writes her poetry in German. Nor is it surprising that, living in Germany, Ghanaian Amma Darko composes her novels in that same language. After abandoning Prague for Paris in 1975, Milan Kundera continued creating fiction in his native Czech—until 1995, when he published *La Lenteur* (*Slowness*), a confection that simulates an eighteenth-century French novel and is written in French.

Immigration is often reluctant, the product of vast historical forces over which the individual has little control. Though she managed to write important poetry in English rather than her native Fulani, Phyllis Wheatley did not choose to be transported from Africa to America, as a slave. In *Lost in Translation*, Eva Hoffman recounts how, at the age of thirteen, she was uprooted from her beloved Cracow by her apprehensive Jewish parents and resettled in Vancouver, where English inevitably supplanted her native Polish, though certain feelings persist—like *tęsknota*, a blend of nostalgia, sadness, and longing—that she can articulate only in Polish. Tom Stoppard departed Czechoslovakia as a young child, and his identity as an English playwright is likewise not a case of individual choice. Nor is it for Kazuo Ishiguro, who was only six when his family left Japan for England. It is not uncommon for a young immigrant—like Yehuda Amichai, Guillaume Apollinaire, Eva Figes, José-Maria de Heredia, Eugène Ionesco, Ruth Prawer Jhabvala, Clarice Lispector, Elena Poniatowska, or Anzia Yezierska—to excel in the language of the adopted country.

More unusual is *Dafydd Morgan* (1897), a notable novel that, though living in L'Anse, Michigan, R. R. Williams composed in Welsh.

Thus translingualism is not always an expression of autonomy, of independence from a culture that forces us to think and speak along its particular lines. However, deliberate to the point of being whimsical are instances of translingual larks and hoaxes—the fictional lexicon that J. R. R. Tolkien devised for his Hobbit fantasies; *The Klingon Dictionary* that Marc Okrand created to sustain the fiction of *Star Trek*; the private *macédoine* of Latin, Provençal, Catalan, and Spanish that Stefan George called *Lingua Romana*; the blend of Latin and German that Saint Hildegard of Bingen invented, along with her own alphabet; or the pseudo-Oriental Gothic *Vathek* that dilettante Englishman William Beckford wrote in French. By pretending that *Candide* was a translation from German, the preeminent language of philosophical discourse in the eighteenth century, Voltaire offered up a lark and a hoax, as Horace Walpole did when he tried to pass off *The Castle of Otranto* as a translation from Italian. *J'irai cracher sur vos tombes* was Boris Vian's own invention and not, as the author disingenuously claimed, his translation of a hard-boiled detective novel by an American named Vernon Sullivan. When Nathaniel Hawthorne pretended that "Rappaccini's Daughter" was originally written in French, by a M. de l'Aubépine, and when Miguel de Cervantes claimed that *Don Quixote* came from the Arabic of Cide Hamete de Benengeli, each was merely counterfeiting translingualism.

However, Manuel Puig did abandon his native Spanish for one English novel, *Eternal Curse on the Reader of These Pages*—almost, it seems, just to prove he could do it. He later reworked the book himself, as *Maldiciòn eterna a quien lea estas páginas*. It appeared in print in 1980, two years before an English version that reworked both the original English manuscript and the Spanish translation. Umberto Eco slyly introduces *Il Nome Della Rosa* as "my Italian version of an obscure, neo-Gothic French version of a seventeenth-century Latin edition of a work written in Latin by a German monk toward the end of the fourteenth century" (*Name of the Rose* 4). Unlike Eco, James Macpherson intended to deceive. But his facsimile of third-century Gaelic verse in *Ossian*—the most notorious of all literary hoaxes—is another example of counterfeit translingualism. Emigré Andreï Makine was, by contrast, forced to deny his translingual achievement. In order to interest condescending Parisian publishers in his manuscript, the upstart author, homeless when he arrived in France, pretended that he had translated *Le Testament français* from his native Russian, though he had in fact composed it directly in French.

When Oscar Wilde wrote one of his most scandalous works, *Salomé*, he compounded the effrontery by writing it in French, the official language of *Décadence*. "My idea of writing the play was simply this," said Wilde to an interviewer; "I have one instrument that I know that I can command, and that is the English Language. There was another instrument to which I had listened all my life, and I wanted once to touch this new instrument to see whether I could make any beautiful thing out of it" (Wilde 188). As though he were a virtuoso violinist insisting on startling his complacent audience with a performance on saxophone, Wilde chose French for this one occasion because in part he hoped to disconcert the British. "Français de sympathie, je suis Irlandais de race, et les Anglais m'ont condamné à parler le langage de Shakespeare," he explained, in French, the language of his artistic rebellion and nationalistic *ressentiment* (letter to Edmond de Goncourt, 17 December 1891, Ellmann 351). In 1917, T. S. Eliot wrote four undistinguished poems in French. According to his own account, he undertook the task as a personal challenge and a tactic for overcoming a writer's block: "I thought I'd dried up completely. I hadn't written anything for some time and was rather desperate. I started writing a few things in French and found I *could* . . . I think it was that when I was writing in French I didn't take the poems so seriously, and that not taking seriously, I wasn't so worried about not being able to write. I did these things as a sort of *tour de force* to see what I can do" (98).

By contrast, many of the approximately four hundred poems that Rainer Maria Rilke wrote in French between 1922 and 1926 were quite accomplished and no mere priming of his German pump. But Carlo Goldoni confessed to the failure of his translingual experiment, *La Bouillotte*, a play he tried to write in French rather than Italian. In his *Mémoires*, which he nevertheless wrote in French, the principal language of eighteenth-century autobiography, the Italian maestro explains:

> Je connaissais la mécanique des vers français. J'essayai, je travaillai; je fis des couplets, des quatrains, des airs entiers, et après toutes les peines que je m'étais données, je vis que ma muse habillée à la française, n'avait pas cette verve, cette grace, cette facilité qu'un auteur acquiert dans sa jeunesse, et perfectionne dans sa virilité. Je sus me rendre justice; je laissai là mon ouvrage, et je renonçai pour toujours aux charmes de la poésie française. (*Mémoires* 234)
>
> [I knew the mechanism of French versification. I had mounted all the difficulties which a foreign ear must experience, and I had selected models for imitation. I set myself to work, and composed couplets, quatrains, whole airs; and after all the pains taken by me, I saw that my muse in a French dress had not that fire, that grace and facility, which an author acquires in his youth, brings to perfection in his mature years. I became sensible of my imperfections and gave up my work; and I renounced forever the charms of French poetry. (*Memoirs* 410–11)]

French was also the prestige language of the Russian elite for most of the eighteenth and nineteenth centuries, so that not only did Tolstoy employ French when he wanted to represent the conversations of the aristocracy in *War and Peace*, but Catherine the Great, born a German princess, composed twenty-seven theater pieces in French during her reign in Russia as an enlightened despot.

For those who do succeed at the translingual enterprise, the creation of a new voice means the invention of a new self. It is not unusual for translingual authors to adopt different names to signify a new identity through language. After Karl Anton Post escaped from a monastery in Prague, he resurfaced in North America as Charles Sealsfield, a prolific author in both English and German. When Karen Blixen wrote in English, she became Isak Dinesen, while Alexander Search was the nom de plume attached to the English poems of the man who—sometimes—signed his Portuguese texts Fernando Pessoa. Brian O'Nolan published in Irish Gaelic as Myles na gCopaleen and in English as Flann O'Brien. Kamala Das writes English poetry under that name and Malayalam fiction under the pseudonym Madhavikutti. Writing poetry in French transformed Pauline Tarn into Renée Vivien. Peggy Eileen Whistler became Welsh poet Margiad Evans, and Christopher Murray Grieve wrote in Scots as Hugh MacDiarmid. When the Romanian Jew Paul Antschel began composing poetry in German, he became Paul Celan. Having ceased to write in Yiddish, Shmuel Yosef Czaczkes renamed himself S. Y. Agnon, after the title of the first important work he published in Hebrew, the short story "Agunot" (Forsaken wives).

The most striking case of a self reinvented through translingualism, however, is that of Frederick Philip Grove. When he died in 1949, Grove was read and respected as a Canadian prairie novelist, though it was not until 1973 that D. O. Spettigue revealed in his *FPG: The European Years* an earlier identity that Grove had neglected to mention. In his 1946 autobiography, *In Search of Myself*, Grove makes mythomaniacal claims that his father was Swedish and his mother Scots and that he spoke English, French, German, Italian, and Arabic and read Latin, Greek, Sanskrit, Spanish, and Swedish. In fact, however, Spettigue discovered that the novelist was born in Prussia in 1879 and was the same man who had published fiction, poetry, criticism, and translations in German under the byline Felix Paul Greve. Plagued by debts, for which he even served a prison sentence, Greve feigned a suicide in 1909 and resurfaced in Winnipeg in 1912, writing in English under the new name Grove.

All of this suggests translingualism as a form of self-begetting, as the willed renovation of an individual's own identity. Elias Canetti—who came to German after Ladino, Bulgarian, and English—entitled the first volume of his 1977 autobiography *Die gerettete Zunge* (*The Tongue Set Free*), and he, like many other translinguals, projects at least the illusion of liberty at the buffet of Babel. Whether Stefan George, who mixed languages in his own esoteric blend, became a German or a French poet was, according to what he told Ernst Robert Curtius, a matter of a conscious decision: "Es gab einen Moment, da stand ich vor der Enscheidung, ob ich deutscher oder französischer Dichter werden wollte" (quoted in Curtius, *Kritische Essays* 154) [There was a moment when I was undecided whether I wished to become a French or a German poet] (Curtius, *Essays on European Literature* 125). Though the

Swiss poet C. F. Meyer, too, might have opted for either French or German, he chose to align himself permanently with the legacy of Hölderlin and Novalis.

The most securely canonized of modern translinguals, Joseph Conrad appears to have opted as a sovereign adult to write in English rather than French or Polish. Ngugi wa Thiong'o, who wrote in English as James Ngugi before returning to his native language, Gikuyu, was drawn to Conrad as a secret sharer of the translingual enterprise: "I think what is interesting about Conrad is this very factor," declares the Kenyan, "that he was able to beat a language which was not his own into various shapes to give . . . well . . . meaning to the physical and moral world around him" (Ngugi wa Thiong'o, Interview 126). However, Conrad's own testimony is more ambiguous. He responded with indignation to the legend that he willed himself into being an English author, substituting instead a supernatural myth of linguistic possession. "English was for me neither a matter of choice nor adoption," insists Conrad in *A Personal Record* (1912): "The merest idea of choice had never entered my head. And as to adoption—well, yes, there was adoption; but it was I who was adopted by the genius of the language, which directly I came out of the stammering stage made me its own so completely that its very idioms I truly believe had a direct action on my temperament and fashioned my still plastic character" (vii).

We have already noted some of the calques, the interference from Polish and French in the vocabulary and syntax of a language that, despite the author's assertions, did not manage to make Conrad completely its own. Perhaps Conrad doth protest too much when he goes on to contend: "All I can claim after all those years of devoted practice, with the accumulated anguish of its doubts, imperfections and falterings in my heart, is the right to be believed when I say that if I had not written in English I would not have written at all" (*Personal Record* viii). Even that claim must be qualified: Conrad did write letters, at least, in fluent French, and one of his correspondents, Paul Valéry, quotes him in a statement that appears to contradict his assertion of a quasi-mystical call to write in English and nothing else: "I know French well enough to write in that language also—in a very personal style, of course" (quoted in Megroz 40).

Of course, style is essential to the literary art, and language shapes style. If *le style c'est l'homme même*, translingualism reconfigures style and makes of a single author a multiple man or woman. Studying how the peculiar ways in which the Hopi language organizes tense dictates its speakers' orientation toward time, Edward Sapir famously declared that "Human beings are very much at the mercy of the particular language which has become the medium of expression for their society" (209).

The doctrine of linguistic determinism has been denounced by many linguists, not least the disciples of Noam Chomsky, who insist that universal deep structures subsuming every language are more crucial than superficial differences. For them, translingualism might be an impressive parlor trick but not especially a feat of cognitive emancipation or enlargement. "The important thing," contends Raja Rao, a Mysore Brahman who writes fiction in English, "is not what language one writes in, for language is really an accidental thing. What matters is the authenticity of experience, and this can generally be achieved in any language" ("Raja Rao" 147). When the pope stands on his balcony and blesses the multitudes assembled below in St. Peter's Square, he traditionally does so in several dozen different languages. For the purposes of benediction, language becomes merely instrumental, and we are supposed to assume that the pontiff, who should not play linguistic favorites, is saying precisely the same thing again and again and again.... If the most fundamental modes of thinking and feeling are preverbal, then it becomes a very paltry matter whether on any given occasion we choose to express ourselves in Cherokee or Finnish. Multilingual salutation of tourists in St. Peter's Square becomes merely a matter of mechanics not semiotics.

But to those who savor the textures and resonances of words themselves, every syllable is, like a snowflake, unique, and what the pope says in Latin could never be identical to what he says in Polish, or English, or Vietnamese, or Arabic. Preoccupied with the nuances of the particular verbal system in which they happen to be working, few other translinguals share Rao's and the Vatican's nonchalance toward language choice. It hardly seems "an accidental thing" that Celan wrote his stark poetry not in Romanian, Russian, or French but in German, the language of the brutes who had incarcerated him and exterminated his people. Refusing to be constrained by the structures of any single language, translinguals seem both to acknowledge and to defy the claims of linguistic determinism. It is precisely because they recognize the power of particular languages that they attempt to transcend them. In *Le Schizo et les langues* (1971), Louis Wolfson, a native New Yorker hospitalized for schizophrenia, records in brilliant French and fragments of Russian, German, Hebrew, and other languages his psychotic rejection of his mother's—and his father's—tongue, the one that he was reared to speak: English.

For Canetti, philology can be a form of philandering. Those who flirt with different languages are inconstant lovers. Twenty-three years after his father's unexpected death from a heart attack, Canetti, who had been seven at the time, learned from his mother that her linguistic waywardness had actually killed his father. Alone in the spa of Bad Reichenhall for a summer rest cure, Canetti's mother had been wooed by a handsome doctor. When she returned to the family home in Manchester, her husband, intensely jealous, interrogated her about her behavior, which evidently had consisted of nothing more perfidious than talk—but in German, the language that, amid all the other ambient tongues, had been the special link between husband and wife. Canetti now understood that his mother was guilty of linguistic adultery and that this treachery was what had attacked his father's heart:

> I was amazed at her failure to realize what she had done. Her infidelity had consisted in speaking German, the intimate language between her and my father, with a man who was courting her. All the important events of their love life, their engagement, their marriage, their liberation from my grandfather's tyranny, had taken place in German. Possibly she had lost sight of this because in Manchester her husband had taken so much trouble to learn English. But he was well aware that she had reverted passionately to German, and he had no doubt of what this must had led to. (*Memoirs* 755)

Canetti leaves little doubt that his mother's translingual transgression, her willingness to speak German with another man, was what caused his father's sudden demise.

Sapir's protégé Benjamin Lee Whorf proclaimed: "We dissect nature along lines laid down by our native languages" (213). But, using French to flaunt ancient aberrations in his stage play *Salomé*, a roguish Oscar Wilde delighted in crossing those lines. So did Breyten Breytenbach when he resorted to English and French to flout the racist mind set of his native Afrikaans. So did Anton Shammas, an Israeli Arab, when he wrote his 1986 novel *Arabesques* in Hebrew. Although he had earlier published a volume of poetry in Arabic and had begun writing *Arabesques* in Arabic, too, he soon turned to what he has called his "stepmother tongue" as the appropriate medium for the book. A metafiction about the family of a character named Anton Shammas—who, like the author, was born into a Christian clan in a Galilee village—*Arabesques* examines the complex identity of a writer living as a member of one Israeli minority within another minority, the Muslims. Responding to an interviewer in English, Shammas suggested that his employment of Hebrew is a distancing device, a liberation from the confines of community: "You cannot write about the people whom you love in a language that they understand; you can't write freely. In order not to feel my heroes breathing down my neck all the time, I used Hebrew" ("My Case" 48). Though assailed for employing colonial languages, African authors such as Chinua Achebe, Camara Laye, Es'kia Mphahlele, and Wole Soyinka might well also respond that they cannot write about the people they love in a language that they understand, or at least that love is most free when expressed obliquely.

A freedom similar to Shammas's is felt by speakers of contemporary Hebrew when they resort to Arabic or Yiddish idioms to express profanities rather than sully the sacred tongue or when parents invent private euphemisms to enable their children to talk about bodily functions. Insult, imprecation, and obscenity are less stressful when expressed in a language in which we have less invested. So are love and reverence. The Latin Mass retains its power for many Catholics who do not speak the language, precisely because, unsullied by quotidian purposes, Latin is a language preserved for the sacred. The narrator of David Plante's *The Accident*—a French American in Belgium, studying theology at the Catholic University of Louvain—recalls the connection he felt as a child between holiness and the French language. And he resorts temporarily to French to evoke those sublime, elusive feelings unavailable to him in his everyday English: "*Quand j'étais* jeune, je priais à Dieu en français, la langue de ma réligion nord-américaine. Dieu, je croyais, ne pouvait pas comprendre anglais, la langue de ma vie quotidienne, la langue de mes jeux, mais ainque ce français que parlaient M. le curé de sa chaire et les bonnes femmes dans le foyer de l'église" (29) [When I was young, I prayed to God in French, the language of my North American religion. God, I believed, could not understand English, the language of my ordinary life, the language of my games, but only the French spoken by the priest from his pulpit and the pious women at the entrance to the church (my translation)].

Second languages are masks that enable us to mingle more comfortably at the ball. The narrator of Maurice Blanchot's novel *L'Arrêt de mort* (*Death Sentence*) explains how, despite his aversion to marriage and declarations, he is induced to propose to a woman named Nathalie—a professional translator of English, German, and Russian—by speaking to her in her (unnamed) native language. Just as Nathalie is transformed by speaking his language, French, he becomes a different person by speaking hers, haltingly:

> [E]lle ne la parlait pour ainsi dire jamais, du moins avec moi, et cependant, si je commençais à ânonner, à lier ensemble des termes maladroits, à former des locutions impossibles, elle les écoutait avec une sorte de gaieté, de jeunesse, et à son tour elle me répondait en français, mais un français différent du sien, plus enfantin et plus bavard, comme si sa parole fût devenue irresponsable, à la suite de la mienne, employant une langue inconnue. Et il est vrai que, moi aussi, je me sentais irresponsable dans cet autre langage, si ignoré de moi; et ce que je n'aurais jamais dit, ni pensé, ni même tu à partir des mots véritables, ce balbutiement irréel, d'expressions à peu près inventées, et dont le sens se jouait à mille lieues de ma tête, me l'extorquait, m'invitait à le faire entendre, me donnait, à l'exprimer, une petite ivresse qui n'avait plus conscience de ses limites et allait hardiment au-delà de ce qu'il fallait. (*L'Arrêt de mort* 99–100)

> [(S)he never actually spoke it, at least not with me, and yet if I began to falter, to string together awkward expressions, to form impossible idioms, she would listen to them with a kind of gaiety, and youth, and in turn would answer me in

French, but in a different French from her own, more childish and talkative, as though her speech had become irresponsible, like mine, using an unknown language. And it is true that I too felt irresponsible in this other language, so unfamiliar to me; and this unreal stammering, of expressions that were more or less invented, and whose meaning flitted past, far away from my mind, drew from me things I never would have said, or thought, or even left unsaid in real words; it tempted me to let them be heard, and imparted to me, as I expressed them, a slight drunkenness which was no longer aware of its limits and boldly went farther than it should have. (*Death Sentence* 61–62)]

Anglophones often find it easier to say either *merde* or *te amo* than their English equivalents. For all the coarseness of contemporary culture, it is doubtful that many of the young Americans who sport chic T-shirts inscribed "Voulez-vous coucher avec moi?" would dare wear one emblazoned with the equivalent in English. Halfway through *Der Zauberberg*, Thomas Mann provides an oasis of French amid more than eight hundred pages of German type. In a Swiss sanatorium during Walpurgisnacht, Hans Castorp declares his love to Clawdia Chauchat in French, though he is German and she is Russian. Castorp explains his choice of language: "Moi, tu le remarques bien, je ne parle guère le français. Pourtant, avec toi je préfère cette langue à la mienne, car pour moi, parler français, c'est parler sans parler, en quelque manière,— sans responsabilité, ou comme nous parlons en rêve" (407) [You of course notice that I scarcely speak French. However, with you I prefer that language to mine, because for me to speak French is in a way to speak without speaking—without responsibility, or the way we speak in a dream (my translation)]. Castorp asks her "Tu comprends?" And any reader who has used a foreign language as a device for expressing what cannot be said otherwise will surely understand. Uncertain what to call the devastating atomic bomb whose development he had directed, J. Robert Oppenheimer, who spoke half a dozen languages, referred to it as *merde*—as though trying to express ineffable horror in his native English might have made the device even more obscene, or at least crude.

If extrication is liberation, then use of another language frees the speaker from the tyranny of a specific syntactical structure. Asked why, after publishing two novels in English—*Locos* (1936) and *Chromos* (1990)—Felipe Alfau reverted to his native Spanish to compose a volume of poetry, *Sentimental Songs / La poesía cursi* (1992), the émigré Spaniard replied: "The poems I wrote in my mother tongue because poetry is too close to the heart, whereas fiction is a mental activity, an invention, something foreign, distant" ("Anonymity" 149). Distance may or may not make the heart grow fonder, but translingualism is a distancing device with coronary consequences.

The emancipatory detachment of writing in another tongue is probably an important factor in the decision of Samuel Beckett, a prodigy of English prose, to become a French novelist and playwright when he was in his forties. As much as his relocating from Dublin to Paris, writing in French (a language he learned as a schoolboy) was a way for Beckett to disengage himself from both Ireland and the onerous example of his mentor, James Joyce. Beckett praised both Joyce and Dante for in effect creating their own languages (see "Dante . . . Bruno"), and the most often quoted of the several reasons that he gave for his translingualism is that: "en français c'est plus facile d'écrire sans style" (Gessner 32n.). Beckett's French is not without style, but it did demand from him a new austerity, a discipline to bridle his unruly English. In a study of Beckett's English and French fiction, Raymond Federman, who himself writes fiction in both French and English, contends that Beckett's move to French was prompted by the creative impasse he had arrived at in his last English book, *Watt*, and a desire to restrain his native verbal profligacy. "It is recognized," says Federman, "that the French language, with its demand for clarity and precision, its strict grammatical structure, its words that always relate exactly to the concepts they describe, does not allow a writer to say what he does not want to say" (*Journey into Chaos* 15). Thus, by exchanging English for French, does Beckett choose his own bondage. Early in *Molloy*, Beckett's narrator endorses Flemish philosopher Arnold Geulincx's conception of free will as the leeway of a slave to crawl east on a boat sailing west. And it might be that facility in switching languages offers just such an illusion of liberation—unless there be some way of crawling entirely beyond the shadows of what Frederic Jameson has called "the prisonhouse of language."

It is hard to take words for granted when writing in a foreign language. Translinguals represent an exaggerated instance of what the Russian formalists maintained is the distinctive quality of *all* imaginative literature: *ostranenie*, "making it strange." Most readers of *Jasmine* (1989), by Bharati Mukherjee—a translingual who, though born in Calcutta, writes in English and not Bengali—are likely so accustomed to indoor plumbing that they take it quite for granted. Yet when Jyoti, an indigent refugee from rural Hasnapur, takes a shower in New York, marveling at how "Touching a tap and having the water hot-hot, and plentiful, was still a sensual thrill" (Mukherjee 175), something ordinary is made thrilling to the reader too. But more than just hot water, a familiar language can also be made to seem foreign.

"The technique of art is to make objects 'unfamiliar,'" writes Victor Shklovsky, "to make forms difficult, to increase the difficulty and length of perception because the process of perception is an aesthetic end in itself and must be prolonged. *Art is a way of experiencing the artfulness of an object; the object is not important*" (754). Working with a strange language is an obvious way to defamiliarize verbal expression, and the work of translinguals, more so than that of most other writers, foregrounds and challenges its own medium—creates the impediment to fluency that is the hallmark of the aesthetic according to Shklovsky, Boris Eichenbaum, and Jan Mukařovský.

Felipe Alfau, the Spaniard who switched to English as the medium of his fiction, begins his second novel, *Chromos*, with observations on the opaqueness of its language:

> The moment one learns English, complications set in. Try as one may, one cannot elude this conclusion, one must inevitably come back to it. This applies to all persons, including those born to the language, and, at times, even more so to Latins, including Spaniards. It manifests itself in an awareness of implications and intricacies to which one had never given a thought; it afflicts one with that officiousness of philosophy which, having no business of its own, gets in

everybody's way and, in the case of Latins, they lose that racial characteristic of taking things for granted and leaving them to their own devices without inquiring into causes, motives or ends, to meddle indiscreetly into reasons which are none of one's affair and to become not only self-conscious, but conscious of other things which never gave a damn for one's existence. (7)

By using language that will not allow us to take anything for granted, the translingual author is fulfilling those conditions that the formalists established for aesthetic experience. It is precisely the "complications" that set in with his use of English that render Alfau's prose artistic.

The Puerto Rican novelist Rosario Ferré attributes a similar impeding power to her use of a second language. She explains how shifting from Spanish to English forces her to concentrate: "English makes me slow down. I have to think over what I'm going to say twice, maybe three times—which is often healthy because I can't put my foot, or rather my pen, in my mouth so easily. I can't be trigger-happy in English because words take too much effort" (62). Repeated use of a native language automatizes writing, reduces idioms to formulas depleted of expressive power. But a foreign language does not permit the writer, or the reader, to take any phrase for granted. Beckett, whose successive narrators erase their own discourse, is not the only twentieth-century author to project a radical mistrust of words, but by writing in an adopted language, he is able to contest the verbal medium more effectively than most others do. *La Cantatrice chauve* (*The Bald Soprano*), the first play by Romanian-born Eugène Ionesco, baldly foregrounds language as irreducibly foreign; it is a verbal farce generated by the moronic dialogue in an English primer the author had tried studying. The French New Novelist who dubbed this *l'ère du soupçon*, the age of suspicion toward fictional characters and their fanciful dialogue, was Russian-born Nathalie Sarraute.

To translingual authors, no utterance can be automatic. Obliged to concentrate word-by-word on what they put on paper, they also force the reader to be attentive to the vapidness of so much of our verbiage. Arthur Koestler, who changed his language twice, from

Hungarian to German and then from German to English, notes that translingualism heightens one's sensitivity to platitude:

> One curious aspect of it, from the writer's point of view, is what one may call "the rediscovery of the cliché," even the broken heart and the eternal ocean, was once an original find; and when you begin writing and thinking in a new language, you are apt to invent all by yourself images and metaphors which you think are highly original without realising that they are hoary clichés. It is rather like the sad story of the man in a remote village in Russia, who just after the First World War invented a machine with two wheels and a saddle on which a person could ride quicker than he could walk; and who, when he rode to town on his machine and saw that the streets were full of bicycles, fell down and died of shock. (219)

Translinguals are the shock troops of modern literature, and those avant-garde movements that, like dadaism, surrealism, and futurism, have been most insistent on the inadequacy and treachery of conventional speech, have been led by multilinguals, translinguals, and other unmoored cosmopolitans. In the work of Hans (Jean) Arp, for example, the Alsatian multimediator who moved as freely between German and French as between painting and sculpture, language becomes opaque, problematic, the subject as much as the medium.

In "Dedication," the opening poem in the volume *Bilingual Blues: Poems, 1981–1994*, bilingual Cuban-American Gustavo Pérez Firmat states:

> The fact that I
> am writing to you
> in English
> already falsifies what I
> wanted to tell you.

While recognizing that this second language distorts his thoughts, Pérez Firmat nevertheless acknowledges the paradox that the linguistic alienation is a natural condition:

> My subject:
> how to explain to you
> that I
> don't belong to English
> though I belong nowhere else.
> (Bilingual Blues 3)

Junot Díaz, who was seven and unacquainted with English when he left the Dominican Republic for the United States, demonstrates similar creative alienation from his adopted literary medium. And he appropriates Pérez Firmat's poem as epigraph to his own first book, a collection of stories in English called *Drown* (1996). Alfau, who moved to New York from Spain in 1916, wrote both his novels in English. Ilan Stavans—who translated Alfau's Spanish poetry into English and is himself an immigrant from Mexico who writes in both Spanish and English—hails Alfau's work for its stance outside each language: "It stands on its own as the contribution of someone living in the abyss existing between two realities, in the margin, on the edge.... he is a frontier dweller" (*Sentimental Songs* xi).

Whether or not they are intrepid, solitary pioneers, distance from language at least situates translingual authors as mediators, not only in texts of their own that straddle linguistic systems. A remarkable number of translinguals have been active and important as translators, brokers who position themselves between the language of an author and the language of the reader. As if these projects were an extension of their own translingual program, Paul Celan translated from English, French, Italian, and Russian into German, while Giuseppe Ungaretti translated from English, French, and Spanish into Italian. Shaul Tchernichowsky, who became a major poet in Hebrew—a language he acquired from a private tutor in his native Russia—published influential Hebrew versions of texts from fifteen different literatures, including *Gilgamesh*, Homer, Horace, the *Kalevala*, Shakespeare, Molière, Goethe, Pushkin, and Longfellow, among many others.

In addition to the books that Uys Krige wrote in Afrikaans and English that made him a focal force in South African letters, Krige also rendered many important works from Dutch, English, French, Italian, Portuguese, and Spanish into Afrikaans. Of the eighteen volumes that comprise the collected works of Stefan George, *Gesamtausgabe, 1927–1937,* five consist of translations—works written in seven languages and including texts by Dante, Baudelaire, Shakespeare, D'Annunzio, Verhaeren, Mallarmé, and Swinburne. Vladimir Nabokov's first published book—in 1923—was a translation of Lewis Carroll into Russian, and Nabokov was active throughout his life in translating among Russian, French, and English. He spent several years translating Pushkin's *Eugene Onegin* into English and devoted much time and energy to justifying the very literal, servile approach that he employed in substituting English words for the poem's Russian ones. Nabokov also translated himself. Often with the help of his son, Dmitri, the itinerant author Englished many of his early Russian texts and, late in his career, when he still could not be read legally within the Soviet Union, took on the daunting task of recasting *Lolita* into Russian words.

Other translingual authors who have engaged in notable acts of autotranslation include Vassilis Alexakis, Samuel Beckett, André Brink, Isak Dinesen, and Mendele Mokher Sforim. In these instances in which the translator is also the translated, the resulting text often becomes a bold reconception rather than a humble approximation of the original. Obviously, translinguals are by the very fact of not being limited to their native language better equipped than most others to engage in translation. And they are by definition the only ones capable of autotranslation, an act of personal reinvention. It is not simply Whitmanesque metonymy that insists that who touches a book touches the man—or woman—who wrote it. Authors invest their identities in the texts to which they sign their names, and when they not only vary the languages in which those texts are written but transmute the language of a particular one, they are denying the existence of a stable self.

Drawing on research in neurolinguistics, Elizabeth Klosty Beaujour finds "cognitive flexibility," "tolerance for ambiguity," and "greater awareness of the relativity of things" to be qualities shared by the émigré Soviet Russian translinguals she studies in *Alien Tongues: Bilingual Russian Writers of the "First" Emigration.* These are also among the qualities most prized in modern literature, traits that constitute the "negative capability" for which John

Keats admired Shakespeare. "My intellect has attained a pliancy and a reach that enable me to assume any emotion I desire and to enter at will into any state of mind" (6), proclaims Fernando Pessoa, who demonstrated his plasticity by writing poems in Portuguese and English and in varied voices that he attributed to distinct "heteronyms," authorial personae who have little in common with one another. The "real" Pessoa, like the "real" Shakespeare, must be inferred from the sum total of his creations, a process complicated by the poet's refusal to bind himself to one language or one style. Pessoa contrasts himself with Omar Khayyam, extolling his own chameleon qualities in terms that sound very much like Keats's praise of Shakespeare for lacking a fixed identity: "Omar had a personality; fortunately or not, I have none. What I am at one moment, the next moment separates me from; what I was one day, I forget on the next. Whoever, like Omar, is what he is, lives only in the world, which is external; whoever, like me, is not who he is, lives not only in the external world but in a successively diverse world internally" (Pessoa 121). And whoever, like Pessoa, is not limited to one language is particularly supple.

Translingualism provides the illusion of creating and transcending finite illusions, as if we could simultaneously view the incompatible perspectives of an M. C. Escher visual puzzle. The American critic Sven Birkerts credits "the fact that my first language was Latvian, the language of home, and that immersion in English only came once I was old enough to play with the neighborhood kids and start school" with his acquisition of "what W. E. B. Du Bois in another context called 'double consciousness'" (39–40). Translinguals can walk a straight line and chew gum at the same time. To move at will from Korean to Quechua to Khosa is to partake of the genius of each linguistic system without succumbing to its tyranny. "The new *mestiza*," proclaims Gloria Anzaldúa, a champion of linguistic, and ethnic, *métissage*, "copes by developing a tolerance for contradictions, a tolerance for ambiguity.... She has a plural personality, she operates in a pluralistic mode" (79). But when does pluralism dissipate into entropy? Thousands of languages compete to organize experience; would embracing each mean supremely heightened sensibility or, instead, terminal catatonia? "I am my language," declares Anzaldúa

(59). If so, then "i" is merely minuscule if its language is diminished. The most complete human being would be the one with the largest linguistic repertoire. However, by what factor can one multiply language and still sustain a multiple self? "Then who will solve this riddle of my day?" asks the poet Joseph Tusiani, who emigrated from Italy to the United States after World War II. "Two languages, two lands, perhaps two souls . . . / Am I a man or two strange halves of one?" (7).

The identity—national, linguistic, and religious—imposed by another country, Ireland, seemed too constrained for the cosmic ambitions of James Joyce. "When the soul of a man is born in this country," complains Stephen Dedalus to the Irish nationalist Davin, "there are nets flung at it to hold it back from flight. You talk to me of nationality, language, religion. I shall try to fly by those nets" (*Portrait* 203). Translingualism, whether through the syncretic rhetoric of Joyce's *Finnegans Wake* or his compatriot Beckett's flight to French, is a tightrope act without nets.

3

TRANSLINGUAL AFRICA

For Yvan Goll, the decision to write any one of his poems in either German or French was an aesthetic one, analogous to that of a composer who chooses to create a sonata for piano, violin, or clarinet according to which system of sonic expression seems most challenging to explore at the time. It both presupposes and demonstrates artistic free will. If, according to the Sapir-Whorf thesis, we are epistemological prisoners of the limited possibilities inherent in the languages we speak, then multilingualism is emancipation. It enables us to entertain feelings and thoughts unavailable to the monolingual. Like the sculptor equipped to work with marble, clay, steel, or bronze, the translingual author can exercise the freedom of gratuitous expression, the luxury of exploring a medium merely for the sake of plumbing its possibilities.

However, most speakers or writers who change languages do not share the French Symbolists' concern with the mystical phonology of particular vowels. Language is usually a practical tool, and we sort through tools until we find the one that can best perform the task at hand. Dialogue for El Teatro Campesino is usually written in Spanish, not because of any distinctive qualities in the language but because director Luis Valdez is trying to make direct contact with an audience of Spanish-speaking farmworkers. Jacob Gordin began his career as a writer in Russia and in Russian, but when he moved to the United States in 1891 and wrote for the theater, he turned to Yiddish as the language most effective in reaching working-class Jewish immigrants.

Language is a social phenomenon, a function and an instrument of institutional power, and translinguals also often remind us of the political implications of discourse. In multilingual nations such as Belgium, Canada, China, Finland, India, or Switzerland, the choice of a literary medium is not an innocent act. Those who write in Provençal, Basque, or Gaelic are rejecting the cultural and political hegemony of a language that is frequently the first they spoke. Among Latino authors in the United States, the decision to use Spanish, English, or a raffish, macaronic blend of the two is at least as much polemical as it is aesthetic. As Frantz Fanon noted, "Mastery of language affords remarkable power" (18), and by mastering myriad languages, authors expand their power. The compulsion to conquer multiple grammars might be a symptom of megalomania.

With many colonial and postcolonial authors, the prestige and power of a particular language, its access to an alphabet, a printing press, and a reader have been the principal determinants of translingualism, even—or especially—when such writers are rejecting English, French, Portuguese, and Arabic. Imperial languages exert authority not necessarily because of their inherent virtues. They elicit allegiance not especially because authors are dissatisfied with their native tongues or are ambitious to try something new. Within their large spheres of influence, English, French, Spanish, and Russian have induced authors respectively to abandon Yoruba, Vietnamese, Quechua, and Ukrainian. The Abkhazian author Fazil Iskander began to write in Russian when it was the dominant language of the Soviet Union. Metropolitan languages offer international prestige, a vast pool of readers, and a repertoire of styles and genres that might be lacking in local tongues.

Though he declared his native Italian "unquestionably superior to French in richness, beauty, and energy" (*History* 36), the worldly Giacomo Casanova explains in French why he writes his autobiography in that inferior language: "J'ai écrit en français et non en italien, parce que la langue française est plus répandue que la mienne, et les puristes qui me critiqueront pour trouver dans mon style des tournures de mon pays auront raison, si cela les empêche de me trouver clair" (*Mémoires* 56–57) ["I have written in French instead of in Italian because the French language is more widely known than mine. The purists who, finding turns of expression proper to my native country in my style, criticize me on that score will be right if they are prevented from understanding me" (*History* 36)]. And when French authority waned, Italy became a camp for English authorship—Keats, Browning, Joyce, and Pound, among others.

In the foreword to his first English novel, *Kanthapura*, published under the Raj in 1938, Raja Rao—whose native language was Kannada—voices many of the frustrations and challenges of educated authors from colonial and postcolonial societies who try to express themselves with the vocabulary of their conqueror:

> One has to convey in a language that is not one's own the spirit that is one's own. One has to convey the various shades and omissions of a certain thought-movement that looks maltreated in an alien language. I use the word "alien," yet English is not really an alien language to us. It is the language of an intellectual make-up—like Sanskrit or Persian was before—but not of our emotional make-up. We are all instinctively bilingual, many of us writing in our language and in English. We cannot write like the English. We should not. We cannot write only as Indians. We have grown to look at the large world as part of us. (vii)

For Rao, as for the Tamil-speaker R. K. Narayan or the Ibo-speaker Chinua Achebe, the use of English as a literary medium is a tonically—and doubly—alienating experience. It creates a new persona that is distant from both the native culture and the dominant Anglophonia. Primers and dictionaries used to be as important as swords and cannon to the perpetuation of the European empires. Politics more than aesthetics accounts for the fact that postcolonial authors continue to cultivate translingualism. Subalterns have appropriated the language of the missionary schoolmaster, and, in the memorable phrase of Salman Rushdie, the Empire writes back. Africa offers a vivid case study in how translingualism can be less a matter of choosing from among piano, violin, and clarinet than of selecting a trumpet over a kakaki. Trumpets resound more loudly throughout the world.

The most eminent translinguals of the twentieth century are doubtless Samuel Beckett, Joseph Conrad, and Vladimir Nabokov, but colonialism and dislocation have impelled hundreds of writers throughout the continent of Africa, and in diaspora, to write in a language other than their native tongue. Even during the classical period, when Latin was the imperial language of much of the Eastern Hemisphere, many of those who wrote in it—including Apuleius, Terence, and Augustine—were Africans who spoke another language first. In Africa, claims Neville Denny, there is "a higher proportion of languages in relation to population than in any other comparable region on earth" (quoted in Spencer 40). There is no other region on earth comparable to Africa, and each polyglot region of the world is polyglot in its own way. But India, the Caucasus, and Borneo have certainly also served as intense linguistic cauldrons. Like Africa, they are exceptionally dense with languages and even language families. However, from Egypt and the Maghreb to the Cape of Good Hope, most writers are obliged to make their separate peace with a vast array of ambient tongues. The continent of Africa—resounding to the clamor of approximately one thousand indigenous languages as well as half a dozen European ones, Arabic, and various creoles and pidgins—is an extraordinary laboratory for examining the phenomenon of literary translingualism. One country, the "Rainbow Nation" of post-apartheid South Africa, has certified eleven official languages: Afrikaans, English, Ndebele, Pedi, Sotho, Swati, Tsonga, Tswana, Xhosa, Venda, and Zulu. In the writings inscribed on what Chantal Zabus has called the African palimpsest, even monolingual texts carry echoes of other voices.

Yet the situation is not quite unique to Africa. Achebe's notorious attack on the Eurocentrism he finds in *Heart of Darkness* (see "An Image of Africa") is perhaps all the more severe for the fact that he and the novella's Polish-English author, Conrad, are doppelgängers, veritable secret sharers of translingual virtuosity. Wole Soyinka, who has called for adoption of Swahili as the pan-African language, spoke—in English rather than his native Yoruba—about heteroglossia in Africa at a conference in Stockholm in 1986:

> Nothing is frankly more boring, more simultaneously pompous and pathetic than to have the phenomenon treated like some unique affliction on the face of African humanity. In Europe today, the Welsh and Scots in Britain, the Bretons and Occitans in France, the Basque and Catalonians in Spain, the Georgians and Asiatics in the Soviet Union, the

Turks in Bulgaria all, in varying degrees confront, negotiate and adopt varying accommodations with the situation. (35)

Translingualism is one of the more remarkable accommodations, and, global as it is, it does assume distinctive complexions in Africa.

Any roster of notable translingual African authors would have to include Chinua Achebe, Ama Ata Aidoo, A. K. Armah, Rachid Boudgedra, Breyten Breytenbach, André Brink, Andrée Chedid, Buchi Emecheta, Nuruddin Farah, Abdelkébir Khatibi, Gabriel Okara, Léopold Senghor, Wole Soyinka, Gabre-Medhin Tsegaye, and Kateb Yacine. No less remarkable in that company is Sol T. Plaatje, author of *Mhudi* (1930), the first English-language novel by a black South African. Though his native tongue was Tswana, Plaatje also studied Afrikaans, Dutch, French, German, Sotho, Xhosa, and Zulu. In addition to his original writings in English and Tswana, he collected and translated indigenous folk materials into English and translated Shakespeare into Tswana.

Translingual, too, is Karen Blixen, one of the most widely read writers to have come out of Africa, back to her native Denmark. She adopted both the nom de plume Isak Dinesen and the English language in order to create her vivid Gothic tales. Though Blixen was living in British East Africa and sleeping with an Englishman, Denys Finch Hutton, her desire to create a new identity from and through a different language was a strong incentive for writing in English rather than Danish. According to biographer Judith Thurman, "English was the language of her daily life and of her primary audience and critic, Denys. But she also seems to have chosen it the way she chose to use a pseudonym, as a means to gain freedom through distance, a clearer *Overblik* (overview) and a kind of anonymity" (212).

When John Keats credited great poets in general and Shakespeare in particular with possessing "negative capability," he was valorizing an unusually supple, polymorphous identity that refuses to be chained to any monolith. Karen Blixen demonstrated negative capability in her reinvention as Isak Dinesen, a frontier farmer and Anglophone author. But an even more striking case is that of Fernando Pessoa, a bisexual who alternated between Portuguese and English as the medium for his poetry. He signed his Portuguese works with one of four distinct heteronyms, about which he devised elaborate biographical details: "Alvaro de Campos," a naval engineer educated in Glasgow, writes expansive Whitmanesque lines; "Ricardo Reis," a classical pagan in spirit, employs an austere, epigrammatic style; "Alberto Caeiro" writes pastoral, antiurban poems; the poems ascribed to "Fernando Pessoa" document their author's anxious quest for spiritual fulfillment. There were other, minor Portuguese heteronyms, and Pessoa's identity multiplied further in the English poetry that he composed and credited to the pseudonymous "Alexander Search."

A wit might quip that the five greatest poets of the twentieth century are Fernando Pessoa. His place in African literature is prominent but ambiguous. Though he lived in Portugal for most of his life, Pessoa, whose stepfather was a diplomat, spent most of his childhood in Durban, South Africa. Unhailed at the time of his death in 1935 in Lisbon, Pessoa is now generally considered the greatest Portuguese poet since Camoens, but he is also included in *The Penguin Book of South African Verse* and other collections and histories of African literature.

African translinguals do not take the words they use for granted, any more than do those on other continents. Whether in the elegant French of Senghor or the "rotten English" of the Ogoni novelist and playwright Ken Saro-Wiwa, language is foregrounded, defamiliarized, even challenged. The macédoine of malapropisms that constitutes *The Palm-Wine Drinkard* is oddly more expressive than it would have been if Amos Tutuola had written his 1952 novel, more fluently, in his native Yoruba.

In the taxonomy of African translingualism, ambilinguals include Pessoa (Portuguese and English), André Brink (the only author to have won South Africa's prestigious annual CNA Award separately in Afrikaans and English), Ngugi wa Thiong'o (who turned to his native Gikuyu after producing an oeuvre in English, as James Ngugi), Guillaume Oyono-Mbia (a Cameroon playwright who alternates between English and French), Okot p'Bitek (a Ugandan who writes in Lwo, Acholi, and English), Charles Mungoshi (a Zimbabwean who writes in Shona and English), Gabre-Medhin Tsegaye (an Ethiopian playwright who alternates between Amharic and English), Oswald Mbuyiseni Mtshali (a South African poet who writes in both Zulu and English), and

Rachid Boudjedra (who turned to Arabic after publishing six novels in French). Internal code-switching—similar to the Spanglish of Chicanas Gloria Anzaldúa, Lorna Dee Cervantes, and Sandra Cisneros—can be found in Kenyan novelist David Maillu's macaronic prose, which combines English, Swahili, and Kamba. Translinguals whose principal work is confined to one language include Olaudah Equiano (1745–97)—who was captured into slavery at twelve and went on to become the first black African to write in English—and members of the generation of Africans who emerged just prior to independence: Achebe, Senghor, Soyinka, and others who expressed themselves primarily in English, French, or Portuguese.

Migration is an important factor accounting for translingualism in Europe and the Western Hemisphere. And the vast diaspora created by slave traders resulted in millions of dark-skinned speakers of English, French, Portuguese, and Spanish. But it is colonialism, European domination not only of Africa's economies and politics but its cultures as well, rather than relocation that accounts for most translingualism within the continent itself—the fact that much of its most important literature is written in English, French, and Portuguese rather than Xhosa, Hausa, or Dinka.

Nationalist revulsion against colonialism accounts for another kind of translingualism: the deliberate choice of a language as an assertion of communal identity. Thus did Dante, Geoffrey Chaucer, Joachim du Bellay, and others begin to write in the local vernacular instead of—or often, in addition to—the imperial language Latin. Finnish was effectually born with the 1835 publication of the *Kalevala* and a determination to fashion a national alternative to Swedish. Modern Hebrew literature is largely the creation of stubborn secularists who chose the path of most resistance to write in a language that had not been spoken for virtually two thousand years. S. Y. Agnon, Chaim Nachman Bialik, Shaul Tchernichowsky, and others turned to Hebrew—after Yiddish, Polish, Russian, German, and other European languages—in order to affirm and create a new era in Jewish culture. A similar dynamic accounts for the adoption of Irish Gaelic by writers more comfortable in English and of Basque by writers who spoke Spanish. Decisions such as those by Mazisi Kunene to write in

Zulu and by Ngugi in Gikuyu are an explicit rejection of colonial English in favor of an indigenous tongue. Afrikaans became the embodiment and assertion of white Afrikaner culture, and the fact that one of its first major poets, Eugene Marais (1871–1936), wrote his earliest works in English was a slight embarrassment. But when after examining the manuscripts of his Afrikaans poems, F. G. M. du Toit was forced to conclude that Marais had continued to think in English all his life, it was a communal humiliation.

African translingualism is symptomatic of imbalances of power—political, economic, military, and cultural. The backing of banks, publishing houses, schools, and armies makes some tongues easier to swallow than others. Gikuyu and English lack the symmetry that Stefan George and C. F. Meyer confronted when choosing between French or German. Explaining his decision after publishing *Petals of Blood* in 1977 to turn to Gikuyu exclusively, Ngugi insists that in a genuinely free linguistic marketplace he might not have abandoned English. However, he notes, "English and the African languages never met as equals, under conditions of equality, independence, and democracy, and this is the root of all subsequent distortions" (*Moving* 35).

That meeting of ostensible equals is what inspired Uri Zvi Greenberg to alternate between the templates of Hebrew and Yiddish in experiencing the universe—and Rilke, between German and French. The absence of linguistic equality is what impelled Njabulo Ndebele to write his fiction in English rather than Zulu, Xhosa, or Sesotho, all of which he grew up speaking. "I didn't really choose to write in English," Ndebele told an interviewer, "it was force of circumstance. In fact I started writing in Zulu, but I abandoned it because all the people who fired my imagination, the poets I discovered on my own—Dylan Thomas, W. H. Auden, Louis MacNeice, or the Second World War poets and others like Wilfred Owen, several others; even Dante who I read ponderously in English translation (I was very young, but I kept going and he really fascinated me)—I read in English" (Interview 149). By virtue of their employing English or French rather than their mother tongues for literary expression, most of the most prominent African authors are translinguals, though virtue has nothing to do with it: European languages ensure easier access to publishers and readers.

Choice of language is no innocent action. Endorsements of one verbal system over another have become fighting words in Belgium, Canada, India, Switzerland, and elsewhere. In Soweto in 1976, widespread opposition to compulsory Afrikaans was the proximate cause of riots that eventually led to rout of the Afrikaner regime. "Especially after 1976," insists Hein Willemse, "no black Afrikaans writer can be spared the intellectual anguish of rationalizing his choice of language" (242). Willemse rationalizes his own decision to write in Afrikaans by noting that, though it is the language of the oppressor, it is also the vernacular of the oppressed—a creole that, though of European derivation, originated among slaves who created a lingua franca out of Dutch, French, English, Khoisan languages, and Bantu. Afrikaans is spoken exclusively in Africa and, for all its association with white supremacy, more widely by nonwhites than whites.

Within Africa, no question is more belabored than what are the appropriate languages for the continent's literature. Its multiple answers account for the distinctive directions taken by African translingualism. In 1963, a year after Senghor elegantly celebrated French as "Langue de culture," Obiajunwa Wali proclaimed: "any true African literature must be written in African languages" (14), though he begged the vexing question of just what is an African language. Is there a statute of limitations of a certain number of centuries that makes Arabic African but Spanish European?

Ngugi echoes Wali in insisting that "African literature can only be written in African languages." But he goes on to define the category in extremely restrictive terms as "the languages of the African peasantry and working class, the major alliance of classes in each of our nationalities and the agency for the coming inevitable revolutionary break with neo-colonialism" (*Decolonising* 27). A sense of populist obligation led Ngugi to abandon his translingual career in English and return to Gikuyu, initially to write plays in a language that the local villagers could understand. It similarly led Kateb Yacine, an accomplished author in French, to write plays in demotic Arabic for presentation in rural parts of Algeria. Arguing against any translingualism at all, Akinwumi Isola appeals to the writer's loyalty to his native culture: "Historical conditions largely determine a writer's choice of language, but don't writers have a moral obligation to give something back to the literary ecosystem from which they initially drew their inspiration? Every language deserves its own written literature, and every writer who speaks that language should give something back to it" (25). The implication that translingualism is linguistic treason is itself distinctively African, the product of multilingual colonial societies in which languages were organized hierarchically as emblems and instruments of stratification. No one considers the Italian playwright Carlo Goldoni a traitor or an ingrate for having written some of his works in French.

Historical conditions, though, have forced many important African writers into exile, into countries where Xhosa seldom clicks and it is reasonable to pursue the writing life with tools of the local language. Historical conditions also created a gap between a small African elite, educated in European languages, and the unlettered masses, who often speak several indigenous languages but read none. To reach the majority of their compatriots, African authors resort to the oral media of theater and poetry, in languages not taught in their selective schools. To establish their international literary stature, they write novels and poems in languages that can be published beyond the continent. While it was relatively easy for Ernest Claes to jump between Flemish and German and for José-Maria de Heredia and Fernando Arrabal to bridge the gap between Spanish and French, African translinguals who would address both their native communities and a global public must move between radically different language systems. Tristan Tzara's effort in shifting Romance languages, from Romanian to French, was not nearly as formidable as Kofi Awoonor's task in bridging Ewe and English.

Though born in Somalia, Nuruddin Farah writes in English and dismisses Whorfian anxieties over language, as though precisely the same thoughts could be conceived and expressed in English, Italian, and Arabic, in each of which he is fluent: "I had lots of things to say and *language* did not matter; what mattered was the practicality of putting things down on paper" (quoted in Colmer 131). But for André Brink, language is integral to perception. Though he writes in Afrikaans and English, he argued in French at a conference in Paris: "dès l'instant où l'on se sert du langage pour s'exprimer, on s'en sert dans une tradition donnée, dans une tradition formée par toute une société, à travers toute l'histoire déjà parcourue avant la naissance de cet individu qui s'en sert. Donc pour l'écrivain, le langage et la langue ne sont jamais quelque chose d'innocent" (97) [from the moment that you use language to express yourself, you immerse yourself in a given tradition, in a tradition formed by an entire society, through all the history already elapsed before the birth of the individual who makes use of it. Thus for the writer, language and speech are never something innocent (my translation)].

Rachid Boudjedra, who writes in both French and Arabic, agrees that languages are not interchangeable: "Du point de vue culturel la langue arabe n'est pas seulement un simple instrument, comme toute langue d'ailleurs. Elle est à la fois cela et bien plus que cela. On n'écrit pas innocemment dans telle ou telle langue. Une langue est porteuse d'une culture, d'une sensiblité, d'un sens, voire d'une vision" (quoted in Gafaiti 145) [From the cultural point of view the Arabic language is not merely a simple instrument, like any other language for that matter. It is at the same time that and much more than that. A language is the carrier of a culture, of a sensibility, of a sense, indeed of a vision (my translation)]. And if language implicates its user in the values and vision of a particular culture, translingualism both implicates and extricates. It enables the polyglot to transcend the template of any single language.

Ali Mazrui points to "the emergence of Afro-Saxons in the world" (11), blacks perfectly at home in the language of William Wordsworth and Cecil Rhodes. Yet it is an English inevitably altered to accommodate African perceptions and conceptions, if only to deliver the curse of Caliban in a lexicon supplied by Prospero. Thus does Achebe justify translingual adoption of English as his literary medium by contending that the language is sufficiently malleable to adjust to local conditions: "I feel that the English language will be able to carry the weight of my African experience. But it will have to be a new English, still in full communion with its ancestral home but altered to suit its new African surroundings" (*Morning* 62). When Okonkwo talks in *Things Fall Apart* (1958), the sentences are in English, but they simulate Ibo speech. Zabus calls this "indigenization" and defines it as a "writer's attempt at textualizing linguistic differentiation and at conveying

African concepts, thought-patterns, and linguistic features through the ex-colonizer's language" (3).

Such relexification of imperial English is routinely performed by speakers and writers throughout the margins of the metropolis—in Calcutta, Dublin, Hattiesburg, Toronto, Sydney, and elsewhere. In his 1934 novel *Call It Sleep*, when Henry Roth wants to convey the languages spoken by his European newcomers—including Yiddish, Polish, German, and Italian—but also wants to remain intelligible to Anglophonic readers, he devises a form of English that represents the immigrants' spoken tongues. So, too, does Gabriel Okara's novel *The Voice* (1964) attempt to use English to convey the syntax and lexicon of Ijaw. "There are American, West Indian, Australian, Canadian and New Zealand versions of English," notes Okara; "All of them add life and vigour to the language while reflecting their own respective cultures. Why shouldn't there be a Nigerian or West African English which we can use to express our own ideas, thinking and philosophy in our own way?" (139). In several novels, including notably *Amour bilingue* (1983), Abdelkébir Khatibi uses French to transcend itself and to suggest the collusions and collisions between French and Arabic in Moroccan culture. Translingualism is never complete; in the movement from one language to another, the second always carries traces of its predecessor, explicit or implicit calques.

The most flamboyant of all African translinguals is probably Breyten Breytenbach, who has called himself "the only Afrikaans writing French poet" (*End Papers* 207). A poet and painter who defied South Africa's miscegenation laws by marrying a Vietnamese and who eluded its police, temporarily, by becoming a French citizen, Breytenbach writes in both Afrikaans and English. "All meaning is of course métissage, a new mixture of existing truths" (*Return* xiii), proclaims Breytenbach, a champion of creole. Whorfian in his belief that "The first limits of our thinking are the expressive possibilities of language itself" (*End Papers* 108), he uses English to express his repugnance toward Afrikaans, the language in which he attained literary renown but also the language of the regime that imprisoned him for seven years for collusion with antiapartheid rebels. "I experience a profound revulsion, shot through with pity, when I think of the Afrikaners, when I even hear Afrikaans" (*End Papers* 208), Breytenbach declares—although, hoping to purge the debased words of his brutal tribe, he resumes writing in Afrikaans. A writer who portrays himself as a creature of perpetual reinvention and a paradigm of negative capability, he is optimistic on the matter: "Maybe Afrikaans could be seen as a new avatar of that supple lingo of seafarers, slaves and nomads—of people who constantly have to invent themselves" (*Return* 211). "I am the nomadic nobody" (74), Breytenbach announces in a memoir, *Return to Paradise*—a work that appropriates the words of an earlier translingual, Ferdinand Pessoa, for its epigraph and that later quotes Pessoa's credo: "To live is impossible; to travel perhaps" (74). It is an assertion of the existential mobility characteristic of translingual changelings.

Breytenbach dedicates *Return to Paradise* to yet another translingual, Uys Krige (1910–87), an older Afrikaner who wrote in both Afrikaans and English and translated major works from English, French, Italian, Portuguese, and Spanish into Afrikaans. Explaining his own refusal to confine himself to one language, Krige characterizes translingualism as personal reinvention: "By learning another man's language, you lose yourself to find yourself, you in a sense double yourself, you get a second character or personality—or you at least modify your character or personality, since you come to think and feel like him through your knowledge and understanding of his language. And by so doing you enlarge your field of consciousness, heighten your awareness, increase your powers of perception" (133–34). Panlingualism, then, becomes the consummation of the translingual impulse. From his privileged white redoubt in the South African Cape, Krige was able to put a positive spin on what theologians see as the malediction of Babel, Africanists as a continental problem.

It is unlikely that Samson O. O. Amali feels quite the same exuberance of Proteus when he moves between Idoma, the local idiom, and English, a language more widely disseminated and respected even within Nigeria. But translinguals are the picaros of African, and world, literature—resourceful rogues who soar beyond the radar of separate verbal systems designed to track the universe. In nothing so much as in their linguistic mobility do they personify the trickster of African folklore. Breytenbach advances an avian metaphor to describe his own breed of author and to suggest the paradox that, because of their awareness of the relativity of expression, translinguals are the finest champions of any one language: "The writer flies through language as wide and as unique as his wings. Like all birds he sings in French when in France, Afrikaans in Africa, English in London, and so forth. . . . It's the only way to be indigenous. Those winged creatures who recite the same song wherever they go will soon be picked upon as unadapted moon-growths of a foreign culture, their warbling quenched in a burbling of blood through the slit in the crop" (*Return* 223).

In their study of Franz Kafka, a Jew writing in Prague in German, Gilles Deleuze and Félix Guattari devise the category of "minor literature"—texts written by a minority within and against a dominant culture. By that definition, Kafka's fictions, like those of Richard Wright, are minor literature, but the term surely also applies to many African works, particularly those of translingual authors attempting to express themselves in English, French, Portuguese, or even the secondary Afrikaans, Arabic, and Swahili. In what might be interpreted as a commentary on the phenomenon, Kafka himself imagined how, offered the choice between being a king or the courier of a king, everyone opts to be a courier. He concludes his brief parable "Couriers" by noting: "Therefore there are only couriers who hurry about the world, shouting to each other—since there are no kings—messages that have become meaningless. They would like to put an end to this miserable life of theirs but they dare not because of their oaths of service" (185).

Between Breytenbach's vision of translinguals as zestful, emancipated birds and Kafka's as wretched, prattling couriers, there is no compromise, except in the image of passenger pigeons—a species that was extinct by 1914. Yet translingual authors remain a thriving breed. In Africa, literary translingualism stems from both the curse of Babel, which is responsible for the hundreds of mutually unintelligible tongues spoken throughout the continent, and the curse of Caliban, which is the impetus to master a few in order to revile the oppressor. In this literary calculus, one benefaction eclipses two maledictions.

4

COETZEE READS BECKETT

Before he began writing the novels that established his international stature, J. M. Coetzee was a literary scholar. His doctoral dissertation on the fiction of Samuel Beckett anticipated his later interests as a critic while it demonstrated early, fruitful affinities with an Irish Francophonic author who, like the younger South African, lived between two languages. A review of Coetzee's career demonstrates his debt to Beckett and his continuing preoccupation with linguistic choice as enabler and impediment.

If English is not exactly Coetzee's mother tongue, it was certainly his mother's language. Born in Cape Town, in 1940, to an Afrikaner father and an English mother, Coetzee has distinguished himself—through eight books of fiction, three books of criticism, and a memoir—as one of the preeminent English-language authors in and of South Africa. Though he was educated in Anglophonic classrooms and repelled by what he regarded as the brutishness of Afrikaner culture, Coetzee grew up speaking Afrikaans within his family. Contending that "English in South Africa is what one might call a deeply entrenched foreign language," he explains in his characteristically fastidious English that "There is a sense in which I have always approached English as a foreigner would, with a foreigner's sense of the distance between himself and it" ("Homage" 7).

In his memoir *Boyhood* (1997), Anglophilic Coetzee describes the terror he felt over rumors that schoolchildren with Afrikaans surnames would be removed from English-language classes and that his linguistic imposture would be exposed: "he is filled with panic at the thought of having to move to an Afrikaans class. He tells his parents he will not obey. He will refuse to go to school" (69). For Coetzee, a student of linguistics, language in general—

like English in particular—has long been, in David Attwell's phrase, "a field of contestation" (Coetzee, *Doubling* 8). The relations between words and thought, the boundaries between one language and another, and the limits of language have been central to Coetzee's concerns as both a novelist and a scholar.

Joseph Conrad did not come to English, after Polish and French, until he was in his twenties. Coetzee was speaking English at a much earlier age than this, but he, too, might be classified as translingual, an author whose linguistic medium is a matter of option. And were it not for Breyten Breytenbach's aversion to the culture from which the term and the institution of apartheid derive, the apostate poet might have continued composing his verses in the masterful Afrikaans that made him lauded in the community he rejected. For his part, though Coetzee never even began to write professionally in Afrikaans, he claims to have made a linguistic choice—one based less on politics than on his belief that Afrikaans is "frankly dull" and that English has "a historical layer in the language that enables you to work with historical contrasts and oppositions in prose" ("An Interview" 2). Like the North African Augustine, who resolved to write in Latin, the better to spread his thoughts throughout an unholy empire, the South African Coetzee became a student and master of English, "the greatest imperial language of them all" (*Doubling* 53).

Translinguals are not only a large and important category of authors. As acutely conscious of their links to others within the group as to the problematics of language, they constitute a tradition, not an arbitrary assemblage. The case of J. M. Coetzee is a vivid demonstration of how literary translingualism is in fact a legacy rather than a taxonomic contrivance. Few other authors of his eminence have documented their elective affinities with kindred literary figures as thoroughly as Coetzee has. And translingual authors—particularly Beckett—are those whom he most frequently and fully appropriates.

Ford Madox Ford—the English author who befriended Joseph Conrad and who, spending much of his career in Paris, wrote *The Good Soldier*, which John Rodker wryly dubbed "the finest French novel in the English language" (quoted in MacShane 119)—might be deemed an honorary translingual. Coetzee produced a master's thesis on Ford for the University of Cape Town. After completing his master's degree, Coetzee abandoned academe and South Africa to work in England as a computer programmer. However, after four years in Britain and a nine-to-five job he says he valued chiefly because it left him free to read, he was eager to resume his literary studies. He applied to several graduate schools, and when the University of Texas at Austin—about which he claims to have known very little except that it "had a good reputation in linguistics and a big manuscript collection" (*Doubling* 26)—offered him twenty-one hundred dollars a year to teach freshman composition and pursue graduate studies, he sailed across the Atlantic.

In his 1984 memoir, *Doubling*, Coetzee describes the Austin ambience as "hotter and steamier than the Africa I remembered" and its student population as virtual "Trobriand Islanders, so inaccessible to me were their culture, their recreations, their animating ideas" (50–51). He found himself more at home in the huge library of the university's Humanities Research Center. The archive, which now includes more than thirty-six million manuscripts, happened to house seventeenth- and eighteenth-century accounts of travels to South West Africa by European explorers, settlers, and missionaries. One of these chronicles, written by his distant ancestor Jacobus Coetse, inspired Coetzee to write *Dusklands* (1974), his first book of fiction. The Texas archive, which also contains the largest collection of modern French materials outside Paris, offered Coetzee access to the papers of Samuel Beckett, and his fascination with the Francophonic Irish author led to a dissertation topic for him. In January 1969, he submitted his 315-page study, "The English Fiction of Samuel Beckett: An Essay in Stylistic Analysis." Not only did it help Coetzee obtain his doctorate; it also led him to achieve some valuable insight into the achievements of a formidable translingual author. Though the focus of his research was on *Murphy*, *Watt*, and other fiction that the youthful Beckett had written in English before adopting French as his medium, Coetzee was centrally concerned with the author's style, his distinctive use of language. Awareness that Beckett had abandoned his native language governed Coetzee's study in the English prose, a dissertation he intended as the first installment in an examination of linguistic foregrounding as it occurs throughout Beckett's entire canon.

Coetzee began his analysis with a discussion of Beckett's expressed aversion to "style" as verbal ostentation and with his oft-quoted reason for abandoning English: "parce qu'en français c'est plus facile d'écrire sans style" (quoted in Gessner 32n.). Coetzee credits a desire for control as the motivation for Beckett's choice of French. "The feeling that literary English is somehow a more connotative language than French, and therefore a language less subject to control, or one demanding greater self-discipline in the writer, is not unfamiliar" ("English Fiction" 4), wrote Coetzee—for whom the choice between English and another language is not unfamiliar: he would himself soon be writing exceptionally disciplined prose fiction in English. Coetzee conceded that his current research was merely the first of three stages necessary to a complete understanding of Beckett's style. A description of the relationship of form to content in Beckett's English works, he explained, would need to be supplemented by a similar description for Beckett's French works and then by a comparison of the results. Although he did not use the term, Coetzee was essentially projecting a case study in the phenomenon of translingualism.

Because he did not go much beyond a statistical analysis, replete with charts, graphs, and diagrams, of diction, syntax, and other linguistic elements in Beckett's English prose, Coetzee did not provide that case study in his doctoral dissertation. However, even when comparing successive manuscript versions of *Watt*, Coetzee was animated by what he saw as Beckett's challenge to verbal determinism: Does the language we use necessarily define the thoughts we can have? As Beckett began to move beyond English, Coetzee claimed to find disjunctions between conception and its medium of articulation and communication, as though Beckett were challenging the Anglophonic world order, the constraint of what can or must be generated through English words and word order. The Sapir-Whorf thesis, the principle of linguistic relativity whose premise is that language determines thought, haunts translinguals; otherwise, why would they bother to switch languages? Why else would Kamala Das take the trouble to write poetry in English and prose fiction in Malayalam, if each language did not offer distinct possibilities and limits of expression appropriate to a separate genre? In the case of Beckett, Coetzee acknowledged that an understanding of how English and French respectively compel particular articulations would require genuinely twin texts, in which the author attempts to express identical thoughts in each of the languages. If the premise that language determines thought is valid, such a test is unimaginable. Although there are instances in which Beckett reworked a text from French into English or vice versa, translation, Coetzee noted, privileges one language over another. It is not synonymous with translingualism.

Coetzee's interest in Beckett did not vanish with his departure from Texas for an academic position in Buffalo and eventual repatriation to Cape Town. He has continued to comment on Beckett in scholarly analyses, interviews, and, implicitly, his own fiction. Beckett receives special attention in "Homage," a 1993 essay in which Coetzee pays tribute to "some of the writers without whom I would not be the person I am, writers without whom I would, in a certain sense, not exist" (5). Some of those other writers include Rainer Maria Rilke, Ezra Pound, and T. S. Eliot, each of whom explored the expressive possibilities of different languages: Rilke wrote some of his poetry in French, and Pound and Eliot both made macaronic verse a serious tool of modernism. Although William Faulkner remained monolingual, what intrigues Coetzee about him is the Mississippian's incipient translingualism, his attempt to devise "a formula for perception racing beyond language, language just barely keeping touch with the movement of the mind" ("Homage" 5).

Coetzee paid mind to Beckett in several academic analyses that were published during the years that he was also beginning his own forays into fiction writing. "The Comedy of Point of View in Beckett's *Murphy*" (an essay first published in *Critique* in 1970 and reprinted in *Doubling* 31–38) and "The Manuscript Revisions of Beckett's *Watt*" (first published in 1972 in the *Journal of Modern Literature*, now in *Doubling* 39–42) recycle the stylostatistical work of Coetzee's doctoral dissertation. His essay "Samuel Beckett and the Temptations of Style" (first published in *Theoria* in 1973, reprinted in *Doubling* 43–49) is a brief attempt to do for Beckett's later French fiction what the dissertation did for the early English texts and to provide what the doctoral study had argued was necessary for a full understanding of Beckett's handling of language.

The characters, settings, and situations in Coetzee's own novels are quite compatible with Beckett's bleak, reductive universe. The anonymous magistrate who narrates *Waiting for the Barbarians* (1980) and Magda, the isolated farmer's daughter who addresses us from *In the Heart of the Country* (1977), would not be out of place among Beckett's solitary storytellers, many of whom (like Macmann, Mahood, Malone, Mercier, Molloy, Moran, and Murphy) also commence their names with the letter *M*. Mrs. Curren—the elderly, ailing Cape Town woman for whom *Age of Iron* (1990) is a final, though tentative, testament—endows Beckett's dying Malone with South African coordinates. Michael K, the doltish pariah who, like Molloy, journeys back to his mother's house, is, onomastically, a more obvious child of Franz Kafka than of Beckett, but Coetzee has, while acknowledging the obvious, insisted: "There is no monopoly on the letter K; or, to put it in another way, it is as much possible to center the universe on the town of Prince Albert in the Cape Province as on Prague" (*Doubling* 199). In any case, what seems to interest Coetzee in Kafka—who, while writing in his native German, was a Jew living in an Austro-Hungarian city with a Czech majority—is a veritably translingual aspiration to transcend the template of his medium. Coetzee's tribute to the creator of Joseph K could apply as well to the Francophonic Irishman who conceived *The Unnamable*: "Kafka at least hints that it is possible, for snatches, however brief, to think outside one's own language, perhaps to report back on what it is like to think outside language itself" (*Doubling* 198).

The possibility of thinking outside language itself is what tantalizes the narrator of *Foe* (1986), Coetzee's revision of *Robinson Crusoe* as a metafiction. The central theme and action of this self-conscious narrative is the construction of experience through language, even while the text reconstructs Defoe's eighteenth-century novel through the languages of gender and race. The familiar ordeal of shipwrecked isolation is reconceived through the eyes of a white woman and a mute African slave named Friday. When Susan Barton washes up on Cruso's Caribbean island, she is exasperated by Friday's stubborn silences and his refusal to keep a journal. Baffled by the African, who is incapable of speech because his tongue has been removed, Susan persistently speculates about the obscure origins of Friday's deprivation and about the kinds of thoughts that a man who cannot express them could possibly have.

Foe concludes with the recurrent, haunting image of Friday out at sea strewing flowers in what Susan would like to believe is an arcane ritual commemorating the wreck he alone survived. But she fails in her attempts to crack the semiotic code, and Coetzee leaves the reader with a description of the briny scene in words that attempt to approximate what thought beyond language might be. "This is not a place of words," we are told, as though entering Swift's Laputa, where things refuse conversion into anything but their own immediate physical presence. "This is a place where bodies are their own signs" (*Foe* 117).

It is an extraordinary narrative moment, one that gives voice to Coetzee's abiding aspiration as a translingual—to think beyond a given language and, beyond that, to think beyond language itself. Earlier, in *Waiting for the Barbarians*—a novel whose title echoes Beckett's *Waiting for Godot*, even as it duplicates the title of a 1904 poem by Constantine Cavafy—Coetzee's Magistrate excavates and collects 256 "slips of white poplar-wood, each about eight inches by two inches, many of them wound about with lengths of string" (110). Each slip is inscribed with what seems an indecipherable script. The Magistrate studies these slips of wood, but he is defeated in every attempt at cryptography; he cannot break their code or even confirm that there is a code. When Colonel Joll insists on an interpretation of the slips, the Magistrate offers an ornate allegorical reading so patently contrived as to mock the entire enterprise of semiotics. Perhaps, unlike Freud's cigar, the sticks are merely, defiantly sticks.

Like Beckett's Moran or Coetzee's own Mrs. Curren, the Magistrate would render his life as a report, but he finds himself at a loss for language, unable to communicate with the people who lurk beyond the stockade gates or with the inscrutable barbarian woman whom he is desperate to know. In a dream, his tongue is paralyzed, as futile as Friday's missing oral organ. "No sound comes from my mouth, in which my tongue lies like a frozen fish. Yet she responds" (53), reports the Magistrate, who imagines reaching the woman by bypassing language. "Words elude me" (32), admits the garrulous narrator, who dreams of eluding words into the silence that is truth. "Perhaps by the end of the winter," he muses, "when hunger truly bites us, when we are cold and starving, or when the barbarian is truly at the gate, perhaps then I will abandon the locutions of a civil servant with literary ambition and begin to tell the truth" (154). That truth lurking beyond locutions is a recurrent paradox for Coetzee and other translinguals.

"In another world I would not need words" (*Age of Iron* 19), writes Mrs. Curren, acutely aware that she is recording and creating this world in words. Mr. Vercueil, the laconic derelict she ends up embracing in the novel's final line, is another version of the Coetzee Other, the virtually or veritably mute character, like Friday or the barbarian woman, who makes a loquacious narrator nostalgic for preverbal truth. When Mrs. Curren—a former classics teacher who is fond of etymologies, anagrams, and other ways with words—tries to reason with the unkempt Mr. Vercueil, his response is an eloquent gob of spit: "A word, undeniable, from a language before language" (18). "To speak of this," says Mrs. Curren of the township violence she has witnessed, "you would need the tongue of a god" (99). Coetzee suggests that the lingectomized Friday is no less eloquent than a deity. "Part of being prudent," recalls Coetzee as an important boyhood lesson, "is always to tell less rather than more" (*Boyhood* 29).

Michael K, whose very name is clipped, is effectually mute in a society where racist whites control all discourse. He is spare of speech, and even when he does attempt to say something, Michael K's harelip causes him to emit sounds that his listeners are at pains to interpret. "I am not clever with words" (*Life & Times* 139), admits the obdurate Michael K, brother to Friday, the barbarian girl, and Mr. Vercueil. But that does not discourage others from trying to appropriate his life through their own distorting words.

Toward the end of "the monologue of my life" (12) that constitutes *In the Heart of the Country*, the solipsistic monologist Magda longs for "a life unmediated by words: these stones, these bushes, this sky experienced and known without question" (135). If it could ever be apprehended, such a life would be as irreducible as Friday's flower ceremony or the Magistrate's wooden slips. "I signify something," laments Magda, who envies the density of nonverbal Being: "I stare out through a sheet of glass into a darkness that is complete, that lives in itself, bats, bushes, predators and all, that does not regard me, that is blind, that does not signify but merely is" (9). A child named Piet hands Magda a tax assessment written in two—unspecified—languages (124). The fact that the

South African Coetzee, too, has been handed two languages makes him more alert to the treacheries of words. Even *White Writing*, his examination of the very possibility of a South African literature, conceives of the issue in linguistic terms—"the question of finding a language to fit Africa, a language that will be authentically African" (7).

The numinous moments in Coetzee in which articulation and interpretation are stymied and the narrator accedes to the complex enigmas of unnamable—hence unthinkable?—experience have precedents in Beckett. Consider, for example, the lengthy passage in which Molloy details an elaborate, ingenious system for distributing sucking stones among the pockets of his clothing, only to conclude that "cela m'était parfaitement égal aussi de sucer chaque fois une pierre différente ou toujours la même, fût-ce dans les siècles des siècles. Car elles avaient toutes le même goût exactement" (*Molloy* 113) [deep down it was all the same to me whether I sucked a different stone each time or always the same stone until the end of time. For they all tasted exactly the same (*Three Novels* 74)].

Later in the same novel, Beckett has Moran attempt to analyze the intricate dance that his bees seem to be performing. But the phenomenon defies semiotics, and Moran ends up celebrating the world *an sich*, beyond words:

> Et malgré tout le travail que j'avais consacré à ces questions, j'étais plus que jamais étourdi par la complexité de cette danse innombrable, où devaient intervenir d'autres déterminants dont je n'avais pas la moindre idée. Et je me disais, avec ravissement, Voilà une chose que je pourrai étudier toute ma vie, sans jamais la comprendre. . . . Et je ne saurais faire à mes abeilles le tort que j'avais fait à mon Dieu, à qui on m'avait appris à prêter mes colères, mes craintes et désirs, et jusqu'à mons corps. (*Molloy* 262–63)

> [And in spite of all the pains I had lavished on these problems, I was more than ever stupefied by the complexity of this innumerable dance, involving doubtless other determinants of which I had not the slightest idea. And I said, with rapture, Here is something I can study all my life, and never understand. . . . And I would never do my bees the wrong I

had done my God, to whom I had been taught to ascribe my angers, fears, desires, and even my body. (*Three Novels* 16)]

Beckett and Coetzee contemplate life as a Gnostic mystery, fully aware that it forever eludes their only tool of contemplation: language.

Accepting Ludwig Wittgenstein's dictum that "*Die Grenzen meiner Sprache* bedeuten die Grenzen meiner Welt" [*The limits of my language* mean the limits of my world] (148–49), translinguals resist limits. If, as Benjamin Whorf contended, we organize the universe along the lines laid down by our native languages, they limn alternative lines. What Coetzee found in Beckett, even more than in other translinguals who also aroused his interest, was an author for whom nature and the world are problematic because language cannot be taken for granted. In Beckett, the young South African scholar discovered a tutelary spirit who so respected the power of his medium, whether English or French, that he contested it. Like the Franco-American translingual author-critic Raymond Federman, who is both a trenchant Beckett scholar and a leading metafictionalist in both English and French (see, for example, *Double or Nothing*, *Journey into Chaos: Samuel Beckett's Early Fiction*, *Take It or Leave It*, *The Voice in the Closet / La Voix dans le cabinet*, and *To Whom It May Concern*), Coetzee recognized in the creator of *L'Innommable* a kindred suspicion toward the pretensions of prose. More than two decades after writing his dissertation on Beckett, Coetzee offered this third-person sketch of himself: "As far back as he can see he has been ill at ease with language that lays down the law, that is not provisional, that does not as one of its habitual motions glance back skeptically at its premises" (*Doubling* 394). That wary self-portrait hangs over Coetzee's descriptions of Beckett and over every one of his own fictions.

Coetzee has acknowledged that his first book, *Dusklands*, which counterposes early South African history with the contemporary war in Vietnam, is structurally indebted to *Pale Fire*—the English-language tour de force by Vladimir Nabokov, the most spectacular of modern translinguals. Coetzee paid tribute to the master Russian émigré in a 1971 essay, "Nabokov's *Pale Fire* and the Primacy of Art," that makes its point about Nabokov's aestheticism by demonstrating that Beckett, in contrast, denies the primacy of art. Coetzee's 1973 essay "Samuel Beckett and the Temptations of Style" amplifies his argument about the author of *Watt* by reference to Conrad's similar frustrations with English (see *Doubling* 47–49). Coetzee even discusses Sir Isaac Newton as a latent translingual, a pioneering physicist who, reexamining conventional notions of agency, struggled to dissect nature outside the lines laid down by both English and Latin. He begins his 1982 essay "Isaac Newton and the Ideal of a Transparent Scientific Language" by invoking Wilhelm von Humboldt's theory of linguistic relativity, his proto-Whorfian claim, in the 1830s, that "the national linguistic community to which one belongs becomes a circle from which it is possible to escape only insofar as one steps into the circle of another language" (in *Doubling* 181). Coetzee views Newton as attempting to step beyond circles, "as conducting, with what means syntax offers, a struggle with the inbuilt metaphysics of his language" (167). With gravity to rival Newton's, so, too, does Coetzee.

By 1994 the tutelary ghost of Samuel Beckett seems to have been exorcised. *The Master of Petersburg* marks a departure for Coetzee, not merely in the fact that it is set neither in South Africa nor in indeterminate terrain that could be African. The events in Coetzee's seventh book of fiction all take place in St. Petersburg, Russia, in 1869, and Fyodor Mikhaylovich Dostoyevsky replaces Beckett as virtual Muse. He is even the novel's protagonist. A study in Dostoyevsky's febrile state of mind after he is summoned home from Dresden to deal with the death of his stepson, Pavel, *The Master of Petersburg* is in effect a nineteenth-century Slavic novel written in twentieth-century English—a rival to Conrad's *Under Western Eyes* as the finest Russian novel in the English language. Or rather it is the fictional prolegomenon to a novel already written in Russian, Dostoyevsky's *The Possessed*.

Coetzee imagines the circumstances leading to the genesis of the Russian master's work. Unlike Nikolai Gogol, who chose to write in Russian rather than his native Ukrainian, Dostoyevsky is portrayed as obdurately monolingual despite his recent residence in Germany. "If he were more confident of his French," Coetzee's Dostoyevsky, sexually aroused by his dead son's landlady, assures himself, "he would channel this disturbing excitement into a book of the kind one cannot publish in Russia" (*Master* 134). But Dostoyevsky is not confident enough, and he does not commit translingualism. Instead, he begins to write again in Russian, and Coetzee confronts the challenge of mustering up the Russian master's words in English, of using the template of his own chosen tongue to suggest what might have been thought a hundred and twenty-five years earlier through the Slavic language. The novel's protagonist uses Russian in order to resuscitate his dead son, and Coetzee uses English in order to conceive a life beyond his own.

Used thus, language enables and enlarges empathy, but it can also be a powerful instrument of hegemony. Many of the authors to whom Edward W. Said, in his speculations on the relations between culture and imperialism, returns most frequently—Camus, Césaire, Conrad, Kipling, Malraux, Naipaul, Orwell, and Rushdie, for instance—are either translinguals or anxious itinerants. Many of them adopt the strategy of Caliban, adapting the language of the empire to the purposes of a curse. Said's *Culture and Imperialism* mentions Coetzee only once, and in passing, as the creator—along with Bessie Head, Alex la Guma, Wole Soyinka, and Nadine Gordimer—of a "literature that speaks independently of an African experience" (239). Empire is an explicit theme throughout Coetzee's work, which frequently gives voice to the powerless—the vengeful Boer in "The Narrative of Jacobus Coetzee"; the obsessive and subversive military researcher in "Dusklands"; the young diarist in *In the Heart of the Country*; the Magistrate, who resists the expansionist despotism of Colonel Joll in *Waiting for the Barbarians*; the eponymous simpleton victimized by the military state in *Life & Times of Michael K*; Susan Barton, whose version of Robinson Crusoe is suppressed in *Foe*; the retired classics teacher whose words are ignored in *Age of Iron*. Nevertheless, Coetzee as Caliban has been too covert in his curses to please some critics, who fault him for evading political engagement, for not deploying English as a weapon in a frontal assault upon the racist tyranny of apartheid South Africa. Though generally sympathetic toward Coetzee, Nadine Gordimer, South Africa's only literary Nobel laureate, notes his failure to fulfill the imperatives of her own social realism, his "desire to hold himself clear of events and their daily, grubby, tragic consequences in which, like everybody else living in South Africa, he is up to the neck" (3).

But translingualism sensitized Coetzee to the powers and deficiencies of any system, linguistic or political. To adopt another language is to cultivate empathy for alternative modes of apprehension. A rejection of self-sufficient, totalizing regimes, such negative capability is the most profound form of insurrection. Like Beckett, Coetzee has been able to move from one language to another. Yet linguistic versatility breeds a longing for linguistic freedom, for the chimerical possibility of thinking beyond *any* language. In Coetzee's fictions, all words are problematic and provisional. They are heuristic devices designed to try to capture thoughts that forever outrace expression. At the end of *The Master of Petersburg*, Dostoyevsky begins writing a book as "a trap to catch God" (249). Though the prey will not be caught in whatever language he prays, Coetzee sets his brilliant verbal traps with cunning, savory bait.

5
NABOKOV AND THE PSYCHOMORPHOLOGY OF ZEMBLAN

War, famine, oppression, and technology have combined in the twentieth century to create unprecedented levels of global swarming. And as a result of human mobility, linguistic boundaries have become increasingly porous. Literary translingualism is not a monstrosity and, as we have seen, has even become relatively common. Hundreds of authors have adopted as their literary medium a language different from their native tongue. A smaller number—including Beckett, Brink, Brodsky, Das, Kundera, Ngugi, O'Brien, Pessoa, Rilke, and Wilde—have even produced significant work in more than one language.

However, exceedingly rare is an author who manages to become a major figure in two linguistic traditions. Mendele Mokher Sforim, who pioneered both modern Yiddish fiction and modern Hebrew fiction, is one. But even more remarkable is the achievement of Vladimir Nabokov in two of the three languages in which he wrote prose. He described his privileged upbringing in czarist Russia as that of "a perfectly normal trilingual child in a family with a large library" (*Strong Opinions* 43). By 1938, when he began writing his first book in English, *The Real Life of Sebastian Knight*, Nabokov was—under the nom de plume V. Sirin, the émigré author of *Invitation to a Beheading* (1935), *Despair* (1936), and *The Gift* (1938)—already among the most brilliant Russian novelists of the twentieth century. After Nabokov ceased being Sirin, his subsequent novels—including *Lolita* (1955), *Pnin* (1957), *Pale Fire* (1962), and *Ada* (1969)—earned him a separate position in the Anglophonic canon. Asked which of his three childhood languages he considered most beautiful, Nabokov replied: "My head says English, my heart, Russian, and my ear, French" (*Strong*

Opinions 49). His output in French is sparse and slight, but Nabokov could write quite adroitly with either his head or his heart. And the evidence of "Mademoiselle O," the solitary entry in *The Stories of Vladimir Nabokov* that is written in French, does not refute its author's conviction that, had he not been forced to flee Paris in 1940, he could have grown a Gallic ear: "I might have been a great French writer" (quoted in Field 141).

"The ambidextrous universe" of Vladimir Nabokov, to use D. Barton Johnson's words, not only testifies to extraordinary mastery of two very different languages. Through neologism, paranomasia, anagrams, acrostics, palindromes, alliteration, and other verbal play, it also foregrounds language itself—as a crucial element in literary composition and as a cognitive problem. In no Nabokov novel is language itself so much at issue as in *Pale Fire*, where tenebrous lexical systems construct a poem, contrive its exegesis, and leave a gaping gap between the two. "We think not in words but in shadows of words" (*Strong Opinions* 30), Nabokov told an interviewer in 1963, a year after publishing the book of his that is most intent on recording the penumbral traces of language. If the verbal transparency of Albert Camus's lucid *L'Etranger* constitutes, according to Roland Barthes, *le degré zéro de l'écriture*, then the ostentatious artifice of Nabokov's *Pale Fire* represents the nth degree of writing. The novel's self-consciousness about its own medium is compounded exponentially by means of an imaginary language, Zemblan.

Surrounding and appropriating the four cantos of "Pale Fire"—John Shade's autobiographical meditation in nine hundred ninety-nine lines of heroic couplets—is the critical apparatus provided by Charles Kinbote, a neighbor of the poet in the college town of New Wye. Like Shade, Kinbote is on the faculty of Wordsmith College, where, he claims, as though it were as unexceptionable as the Russian taught by the "martinet" (*Pale Fire* 155) Professor Pnin, he teaches Zemblan. (Readers familiar with the fictional pedagogue Timofey Pnin from Nabokov's earlier novel *Pnin*, where he is anything but a martinet, might marvel at his recruitment here ostensibly to reinforce the book's "reality"). Kinbote reads Shade's poem as a veiled account of the critic's own life as a patriotic native of Zembla forced into painful exile from the "distant northern land" (315) he loves. Scattered throughout the commentary are specimens of Kinbote's mother tongue. We are asked to accept the phrases as instances of the king's Zemblan, since Kinbote insists that he is in fact Charles the Beloved, the ousted sovereign of Zembla.

Pale Fire is not Nabokov's first attempt at *ulogian* fiction—an alternative universe whose local language is not dreamt of by Berlitz. The Russian short story "Terra Incognita" (1931) recounts an entomological expedition into an imaginary jungle where the natives speak Badonian, a tongue unintelligible to the narrator Vallière and his European companion Gregson. In "Solus Rex" (1940), another Russian text that survives as the fragment of an abandoned novel and that anticipates *Pale Fire*, King K rules over a distant northern island called Ultima Thule. The royal family motto, *sassed ud halsem*—translated as "see and rule" (*Stories* 523)—could, by a foreigner, be mistaken for Zemblan. *Bend Sinister* (1947), which was the first novel Nabokov wrote in the United States and which he considered calling *Solus Rex* as well, takes place in a fictional European city whose citizens speak a blend of German and Russian. Even *Pnin* makes passing reference to a "poor, one-lunged" language teacher named Olga Krotki who, at the wartime Intensive Language School, "had to teach Lethean and Fenugreek" (148). But this is less a matter of inventing two languages than of reimagining Latin and Greek forgotten among the urgencies of modern life.

Our exposure to Zemblan is more extensive than to any of these other languages. Within his maniacally elaborate notes to "Pale Fire," Kinbote includes numerous individual Zemblan words, mostly nouns—among them, *grados*, translated as "tree" (93); *alfear*, as "uncontrollable fear caused by elves" (143); *muderperlwelk*, as "iridule" or "iridescent cloudlet" (116); *if* as "weeping willow" (222); and *situla* as "toy pail" (131). It also features entire sentences in Zemblan—for example, *Yeg ved ik*, translated as "I know not" (132)—and even two lines translated from Andrew Marvell's "The Nymph Complaining for the Death of Her Fawn": "Had it lived long it would have been / Lilies without, roses within" is rendered into Zemblan as "*Id wodo bin, war id lev lan, / Indran iz lil ut roz nitran*" (242).

The languages of Zembla and Ultima Thule—in the story "Solus Rex"—are, according to their inventor, "of a phony Scandinavian type" (*Strong Opinions* 91). Like Finland or one of the Baltic nations, Zembla is neighbor to a large, oppressive, and aggressive country that Kinbote sometimes identifies as Sosed and sometimes as Russia. And Zemblan is quite distinct from Russian. Priscilla Meyer reads *Pale Fire* as an allegory of Russian, Scandinavian, and Anglo-Saxon cultural histories and Zembla as a fusion of linguistic traditions: "By constructing the Zemblan language as a synthesis of Slavic and Germanic roots, Nabokov merges his Russian and English childhoods, his Russian and Anglo-American cultural strains, in the regal realm of the imagination" (88). After a specifically linguistic analysis of Zemblan, John R. Krueger concludes: "On the basis of evident cognates and grammatical forms, Zemblan appears to be a West Germanic language with overlays of Scandinavian (Swedish) and Slavic (Russian) borrowings, a few Romance words and a few words in which cognates are not apparent to the writer of these lines" (44–45).

However, Nabokov does not provide enough extended specimens of Zemblan to enable a linguist to do much more than identify morphemes and speculate over cognates. The scholar of Klingon, the language invented by Marc Okrand for Lieutenant Worf[!], a character in the second generation of *Star Trek*, can scrutinize an elaborate lexicon, *The Klingon Dictionary* (1995), and can even study an audiotape of *Conversational Klingon* (1992). But, absent a fluent informant, we must be tentative in observations about the phonology of Zemblan. Nor is there sufficient basis for definitive conclusions about Zemblan's morphology, syntax, and pragmatics, except as they probably mimic those features in the Scandinavian, Germanic, and Slavic languages that it resembles. The fact that languages in the Southern hemisphere of Tlön lack any nouns and that verbs are impersonal and "qualified by monosyllabic suffixes and prefixes which have the force of adverbs" (23) leads Borges to lengthy speculations about the idealistic metaphysics of his imaginary planet. However, Nabokov offers no such correspondence between philosophy and philology. His purposes are different from the social reform that inspired Ludwig Lazarus Zamenhof to invent Esperanto or even different from J. R. R. Tolkien's desire to endow his Hobbit fantasies with linguistic verisimilitude. Zemblan is a symptom of Kinbote's pathological inability to distinguish fantasy from verity, and those who plumb the Zemblan mind by analyzing the language's pronoun distributions, subject-object functions, or structure of tenses exhibit something of the same disorder.

The most significant instance of Zemblan in *Pale Fire* occurs in reference to an egregiously inaccurate translation from English. Kinbote, who confided his preposterous personal story to Shade in hopes that his neighbor would transform it into literary art, had suggested "Solus Rex" as appropriate title for a poem about a solitary, exiled Zemblan king. Pondering why Shade chose "Pale Fire" instead, Kinbote is stumped. What he interprets as an allusion to Shakespeare in line 962 leads him to conclude that the title derives from one of the Bard's plays. Yet Kinbote is thwarted in an attempt to locate the source by the fact that, hiding out in a remote motel room while devising his critical edition of the dead Shade's poem, he has access to only one of the plays, and it happens to be the Zemblan translation of *Timon of Athens* by Kinbote's Uncle Conmal, Duke of Aros. "It certainly contains nothing that could be regarded as an equivalent of 'pale fire,' " notes Kinbote, "(if it had, my luck would have been a statistical monster)" (285).

Of course *Timon of Athens* does contain the words "pale fire," in act 4, scene 3, line 441. Kinbote's luck is indeed statistically monstrous, not simply in the odd coincidence that he happens to have in his possession the one Shakespearean play from which the phrase is drawn but also in the fact that Conmal's Zemblan translation, *Timon Afinsken*, dims the words "pale fire" beyond recognition. In the original text of *Timon of Athens*, the dethroned, misanthropic monarch rails against a galaxy of arrogation and distortion. The words with which Shakespeare's Timon depicts universal theft are:

> The sun's a thief, and with his great attraction
> Robs the vast sea: the moon's an arrant thief,
> And her pale fire she snatches from the sun.
> The sea's a thief, whose liquid surge resolves
> The moon into salt tears.
> (4.3.439–43)

Himself an arrant verbal thief, Conmal has robbed Shakespeare's art, substituting Zemblan words for the author's exquisite English.

When Kinbote in turn translates Conmal's Zemblan back into English, the result is an exceedingly pale reflection of the fiery original:

> The sun is a thief: she lures the sea
> and robs it. The moon is a thief:
> he steals his silvery light from the sun.
> The sea is a thief; it dissolves the moon.
> (80)

Not only does this second-degree translation of Shakespeare lack the crucial phrase "pale fire." But Kinbote—whose sexual orientation would, in 1962, mark him an "invert"—also transposes genders, making Shakespeare's masculine sun feminine and his feminine moon masculine. More ruinously, he robs the lines of poetic power.

Timon's speech describes a cosmos of endless recycling, in which everything is stolen and nothing is original. In Nabokov's universe, where language is identity, translation is a metaphor for general metamorphosis and eternal instability. The imperfection of linguistic transposition is a reminder of the flaws in all communication and of the incommensurability of Self and Other. Nabokov began composing *Pale Fire* while still working on one of his most ambitious projects: a stubbornly literal Englishing of Pushkin's *Eugene Onegin*, along with a massive critical apparatus, that eventually occupied him for most of a decade and filled four volumes. His first published book (1923) was a rendering of *Alice's Adventures in Wonderland* into Russian, and he spent much of his writing career translating back and forth among Russian, English, and French—his own works and those of Yeats, Tennyson, Byron, Keats, Gogol, Lermontov, Verlaine, Baudelaire, Rimbaud, Musset, and Shakespeare, among others.

Kinbote's translation of Conmal's Zemblan translation of Shakespeare's original is as bizarre as the commission that Sergei Rachmaninoff offered Nabokov himself in 1941. He was asked to translate a translation of a famous American poem, for a new English version of a 1913 vocal piece by the Russian composer. Called "Kolokola," it is a musical setting of Edgar Allan Poe's "The Bells" using a text prepared by the Russian Symbolist poet Konstantin Balmont. As Nabokov described the assignment in a 29

April 1941 letter to Edmund Wilson: "Rakhmaninov has asked me to translate the words of his 'Bells' into English. These words are Balmont's reckless translation of Edgar Poe's 'Bells.' But as the Edgar Poem does not fit the music I am supposed to re-shuffle the thing according to Balmont's drivel. The result will be rather uncanny" (*Nabokov-Wilson* 43–44).

The result would not have been any more uncanny than Kinbote's translation into English of Conmal's Zemblan translation of Shakespeare. Or than Nabokov's own experience revising a revision of his autobiography. As published in 1966 and subtitled *An Autobiography Revisited*, *Speak, Memory* reworks material from Nabokov's 1954 Russian text *Drugie berega* (Other shores), which itself was a rendition of the autobiography that he had published in English in 1951 as *Conclusive Evidence*. "This re-Englishing of a Russian re-version of what had been an English re-telling of Russian memories in the first place proved to be a diabolical task," declares Nabokov in the foreword, in an explanation that anticipates the absurdities of Zemblan scholarship, "but some consolation was given me by the thought that such multiple metamorphosis, familiar to butterflies, had not been tried by any human before" (*Speak, Memory* 12–13).

Nabokov's pride in unprecedented achievement manifested itself in regard to his translingualism as well. He resisted comparisons to Conrad, who—writing only in his third language, English, and not in Polish or French as well—lacked Nabokov's linguistic versatility. He distinguished himself from Conrad on two grounds: "First of all, he had not been writing in his native tongue before he became an English writer, and secondly, I cannot stand today his polished clichés and primitive clashes" (*Strong Opinions* 57). Elsewhere, he notes that Conrad "never sinks to the depths of my solecisms, but neither does he scale my verbal peaks" (*Nabokov-Wilson* 253). Concerning Beckett, the other most celebrated contemporary translingual, Nabokov questioned his command of French: "Beckett's French is a schoolmaster's French, a preserved French, but in English you feel the moisture of verbal association and of the spreading live roots of his prose" (*Strong Opinions* 172).

However, Nabokov also disparaged his own success as a translingual author. "My private tragedy, which cannot, indeed should not, be anybody's concern," he stated coyly enough to make it everybody's concern, "is that I had to abandon my natural language, my natural idiom, my rich, infinitely rich and docile Russian tongue, for a second-rate brand of English" (*Strong Opinions* 15). The meiotic effect of labeling the exquisite English of *Lolita* "second-rate" is to remind us of how nonpareil it and an author who can excel in both Russian and English truly are. Deprecating his own English as "a stiffish, artificial thing, which may be all right for describing a sunset or an insect, but which cannot conceal poverty of syntax and paucity of domestic diction," he likened it to "an old Rolls-Royce," when it is manifestly a magnificent new custom-made vehicle. Resorting to a sports metaphor, Nabokov—a polyglot polymath who excelled at soccer and supported himself by offering lessons in tennis and boxing—conceded: "My English is patball to Joyce's champion game" (*Strong Opinions* 56). Vadim Vadimovich, the Anglo-Russian novelist who is the protagonist of Nabokov's last completed novel, *Look at the Harlequins!* (1974), notes that "There has never been a World Champion of Lawn Tennis and Ski" (122). While it is true that, for all his exploits in the National Basketball Association, Michael Jordan stumbled at professional baseball, Jim Thorpe did gain Olympic gold in broad jump, shot put, and two-hundred-meter and fifteen-hundred-meter races, and Bo Jackson and Deion Sanders have each been stars in both baseball and football. Vadim's statement reminds the reader that he, like his peerless author, is a literary champion in two disparate languages.

For all his diverse accomplishments in two such languages, Nabokov rejected the premise of linguistic determinism that our language defines our world. The author who, more adroitly than any other, expresses himself in two languages, insists that we think outside any language. Benjamin Whorf, declaring that "We dissect nature along lines laid down by our native languages" (213), would consign Nabokov to the prison house of his parents' Slavic tongue. "I don't think in any language," counters Nabokov; "I think in images. I don't believe that people think in languages" (*Strong Opinions* 14). Pondering mysteries beyond time and space, John Shade, whose heart attack occasions the mystical vision of an elusive white fountain (which a verbal lapse confounds with "mountain"), chafes at the parochial limitations of language: "How ludicrous these efforts to translate / Into one's private tongue a public fate!" (*Pale Fire* 41). Nabokov shares his poet's transcendental yearnings: "I know more than I can express in words, and the little I can express would not have been expressed, had I not known more" (*Strong Opinions* 45), exclaim the words of the worthy translingual, aspiring to a wisdom waiting just beyond not just any verbal system but all words.

Shade's "Pale Fire" offers up a shadow of Nabokov's plangent personal drama. A Russian Arcadia lost forever in 1917 is defined not so much by wealth and privilege as by habitation in a fertile language. Like his creator and like Pnin, Humbert Humbert, and other émigrés who haunt Nabokov's fiction, Kinbote is forced to abandon a cherished language for one in which he is pathetically maladroit. He confuses the word *halitosis* with *hallucination* (98), for example, and a baseball term with the name of the author of *The Odyssey* (116). If, as Nabokov once suggested, *Lolita* is a record of his love affair with the English language (*Lolita* 318), *Pale Fire* testifies to the trauma of his being rended from Russian. So the Zemblan Kinbote is a thief, snatching his pale fire from the Russian Nabokov, who will in turn derive his identity from the Zemblan scholar if, as Kinbote advises at the end of his commentary, he may next turn up "on another campus, as an old, happy, healthy, heterosexual Russian, a writer in exile, sans fame, sans future, sans audience, sans anything but his art" (300–1).

Despite all his claims about Zemblan, Kinbote might all along have been not Charles II, the deposed King of Zembla, but rather his own anagram, V. Botkin, who teaches Russian at Wordsmith College. On that reading, Zemblan is an elaborate—not necessarily conscious—fabrication that conceals and reveals painful experiences in a geopolitical world contiguous to, not parallel with, the reader's. Kinbote explains that "the name Zembla is a corruption not of the Russian *zemlya* [land], but of Semberland, a land of reflections, of 'resemblers' " (265). The entire Zembla plot is, like the sun's pale fire as seen on the moon, a lunatic reflection of other linguistic dramas. Speaking Zemblan becomes a case of glossolalia and the product not of divine possession but of psychosis.

In his *Le Schizo et les langues*, an intermittently lucid memoir of derangement through language, Louis Wolfson, a native New Yorker living with his mother and stepfather, recounts in studied French his desperate attempts to evade the language of his family and environment, English. For Wolfson—who has devised a private creole of French, Hebrew, Russian, and German, much the way Kinbote concocts Zemblan as an amalgam of Germanic, Scandinavian, and Slavic roots—language becomes a barrier not a link between the self and others. It constructs and confirms his solitude. Kinbote, who reluctantly admits fluency in Russian (*Pale Fire* 268), is, like Wolfson, a linguistic schizophrenic whom the artifice of Zemblan quarantines from the society of those who communicate through natural languages. By the time he finishes writing his grotesque, verbose gloss on Shade's straightforward poem, Kinbote, anguished and alone in a noisy motel room, is as demented as Jack Grey, the escapee from an asylum who, rather than Jakob Gradus, might be Shade's assassin—unless it is Kinbote himself. In the mirror-glass world of Zembla, philology recapitulates pathology.

6

EVA HOFFMAN LOST IN THE PROMISED LAND

"The tongue am I of those who lived before me, as those that are to come will be the voice of my unspoken thoughts" (*Promised Land* 169), proclaims Antin in the adopted tongue, English, that supplanted the Yiddish of her childhood in Polotzk. One of the most vocal of those that were to come is Eva Hoffman, who was also thirteen when she, too, left her native land. Born in Cracow and later transported to Canada and the United States, Hoffman eventually left her native language to write about her life—seventy-seven years after Antin's book appeared.

In *The Promised Land*, Antin recounts how an anxious Jewish girl from a shtetl in the Russian Pale became an ostensibly sanguine American woman. That transformation is conceived largely through language, the novice Anglophonic author's proudly won ability to "think in English without an accent" (*Land* 282). Antin's autobiography is in effect a linguistic palimpsest, an elaboration and reconception of an extensive letter that a precocious fourteen-year-old wrote in Yiddish to her maternal uncle, Moshe Hayyim Weltman, across the Atlantic and that she later translated into English and published as *From Plotzk to Boston* (1899) when she was eighteen. However, the final English version, published as *The Promised Land* in 1912, obscures its author's ordeal of translingualism, the fearful process of acquiring and articulating a new self through a new language.

The Promised Land both embodies and celebrates the metamorphosis of a Yiddish-speaking girl named Mashinke into Mary, the young woman who conquers Boston through English, "this beautiful language in which I think" (*Land* 164). It is the tongue she praises without a trace of treason, of guilt over abandoning her *mama loshen*. In public school the young immigrant excels at

English composition, and she is soon being published by important newspapers and magazines. Extolling the medium in which she has chosen to write, Antin says of English: "in any other language happiness is not so sweet, logic is not so clear" (*Land* 164).

Antin's happiness and life after her initial success with *The Promised Land* and in her Promised Land were to be clouded by chronic, debilitating neurasthenia that required intervals of hospitalization. But in her late twenties, she offers an immigration narrative of unequivocal success. "I am absolutely other than the person whose story I have to tell" (*Land* 1), Antin tells us, and it is by telling us in English that she signals and savors her difference. In Antin's evocation of her family history in eastern Europe, *The Promised Land* indeed provides a fluent English tongue for those who lived before her. Those that were to come voiced different thoughts from those of Antin's fervent faith in the virtues of assimilation. Fin-du-siècle (twentieth century) doubts about the paradigm of the Melting Pot may in fact be "the voice of my unspoken thoughts," the apprehensions about abandoning Polotzk and Yiddish that Antin repressed in composing *The Promised Land*.

Hoffman, who sailed across the Atlantic to a new life in 1959, sixty-five years after Antin, writes in the shadow of *The Promised Land*. Yet the thoughts that Hoffman speaks, also in an adopted English, are not nearly as ebullient as those of Antin. The first of the three sections of Hoffman's autobiography *Lost in Translation: A Life in a New Language* (1989) is an affectionate reminiscence of childhood in the author's native Cracow. Titled "Paradise," it is followed by a section called "Exile" and offers up the myth of Eden and the Fall as a template for Hoffman's loss of Poland and Polish. Born Ewa Wydra, she becomes Eva Hoffman, and the story of the transformation lacks Antin's triumphalism.

In contrast, Antin associates her family decision to go forth from Polotzk with their celebration of the holiday of Passover, of emancipation. She explicitly likens Russia to "another Egypt" (*Land* 7), and fleeing the pogroms and abductions of an anti-Semitic world where "most of the Gentiles were ignorant and distrustful and spiteful" (16) is, for Antin, the story of coming up from slavery into the Promised Land. Not only her book's title but also its chapter names—including "The Exodus," "Manna," and

"The Burning Bush"—posit parallels between her experiences and the deliverance of the Israelites. Hoffman, on the other hand, reports postlapsarian angst over reluctant separation from her native land and language; she is less a Moses than her namesake Eve, writing her story after the Expulsion. An increase in anti-Semitism is the major reason that Hoffman's parents, who survived the Holocaust by hiding in a peasant's attic, decided to desert Poland. But they were emigrants more than immigrants, and when, thirty years after sailing out of Gdynia to Montreal, Hoffman tells her story, she still feels nostalgia for what she left behind, not least a language. And she employs the Polish term *tęsknota* to identify this sad longing—and to indicate that the English lexicon is still not entirely adequate to encompass her emotions.

"I was going on a wonderful journey," writes Antin, a cheerleader for the massive immigration that was dramatically reshaping American demographics on the eve of World War I. "I was going to America" (*Land* 133). In *They Who Knock at Our Gates* (1914), the polemic she published two years after *The Promised Land*, and in numerous articles and speeches, Antin argues unequivocally that immigration was good for America and that America was good for immigrants. It must have been especially painful to her that her native-born husband, Amadeus William Grabau, rejected the Promised Land, becoming pro-German during World War I and then an émigré to China. But Hoffman, embarking on her journey to Canada and ultimately the United States—after America, grown imperial and impatient, had lost its innocence—regards the ordeal more skeptically and wistfully.

Hoffman complicates the trajectory of *Lost in Translation* by recounting a return visit as an adult to Cracow, where she realizes that she does not belong entirely to either world. And in her second book, *Exit into History: A Journey Through the New Eastern Europe* (1993), Hoffman reverses the dominant direction of her first, returning to Europe in 1989 to survey the aftermath of the collapse of Communism. "Every immigrant has a second, spectral autobiography" (41), she writes in *Exit into History*, a book that— by examining the lives of those who stayed behind in Poland, Czechoslovakia, Hungary, Romania, and Bulgaria—offers intimations of what Hoffman's life and her first book might have been like if she had not sailed off on the *Batory* in April 1959. In

Bucharest, Hoffman even commits a heresy against Antin's faith in the ennobling power of American naturalization; she advises Romanians against emigration. "If you go to a new country," warns Hoffman, who went to the New World, "you're bound to have at least ten hard years before finding your footing; why not have ten hard years here, where you can participate in building a new world?" (*Exit* 368). The spectral self lurking behind these words is straining to think in Polish.

At forty-three and with a Ph.D. from Harvard, Hoffman is a more nuanced writer and traveler than Antin, who maintains a fourteen-year-old's exuberance even in the final version of her text *The Promised Land*, which concludes before she enters college. Antin is partial to the poetry of Henry Wadsworth Longfellow, while Hoffman mediates her life through literary allusions to complex authors including Henry Adams, Bruno Schulz, Milan Kundera, and T. S. Eliot. She is especially fond of Vladimir Nabokov, the Russian master who managed to re-create himself in English: "Of all the responses to the condition of exile," she says, "his is surely the most triumphant, the least marred by rage, or inferiority, or aspiration" (*Lost* 198).

But it is the author of *The Promised Land* with whom Hoffman feels the keenest affinity. If Hoffman seems to know so much more than Antin, it is because Antin's autobiography is part of what she knows:

> Among the many immigrant tales I've come across, there is one for which I feel a particular affection. The story was written at the beginning of the century, by a young woman named Mary Antin, and in certain details it so closely resembles my own, that its author seems to be some amusing poltergeist, come to show me that whatever belief in my own singularity I may possess is nothing more than a comical vanity. But this ancestress also makes me see how much, even in my apparent maladaptations, I am a creature of my time—as she, in her adaptations, was a creature of hers. (*Lost* 162)

Born sixty-five years after Antin came into the world and three years before she left it, Hoffman presents herself as a child of a postmodern entropic universe in which heroic energies are dissipated.

Perhaps the most vivid illustration of Hoffman's distance from Antin comes in her experience as an undergraduate at Rice University. Hoffman imagines that by attending college in Texas, in the central time zone of the United States, she might at last overcome her alienation and become a genuine American, absorbed into a campus community that is a microcosm of American society in general. But she finds that she has arrived at precisely the wrong moment for assimilation; in the turbulent 1960s, the culture has become centrifugal, tossing out those who would embrace the center. "I want to live within language and to be held within the frame of culture," says Hoffman, who regrets that her fellow students do not share those ambitions; "they want to break out of the constraints of both language and culture" (*Lost* 194). A decade later, when Hoffman submitted her doctoral dissertation to Harvard University, she took as her theme the grotesque in modern fiction, and what she has to say about the writings of Franz Kafka, Jorge Luis Borges, Samuel Beckett, Nathanael West, Flannery O'Connor, Witold Gombrowicz, and others applies as well to the newcomer's own undergraduate days at Rice: "None of the assumptions that we hold about our reality are sustained; nothing is reliable or stable. Veneers of normality, civilization, apparent order, are stripped off to reveal strangeness, savagery, and absurdity" ("Grotesque" 33). Whereas Antin affirms a stable home in a new country, a new language, and a new name, Ewa Wydra's transmutation into Eva Hoffman is tenuous and incomplete. She writes her dissertation in English, but she signs it "Eva Wydra Hoffman."

Antin, however, pretends to be done with the past, though it is a bizarre claim for an autobiographer to make. As though Mary has definitively displaced Mashinke, one of the family's "impossible Hebrew names" (*Land* 149), she concludes the introduction to *The Promised Land* by contending that the process of writing about her earlier self has been a successful exorcism of it. "I will write a bold 'Finis' at the end, and shut the book with a bang!" (3), she promises, as though books do not continue to trouble their readers and authors long after the final page is turned. And the literary figure whom Antin invokes belies her confidence in the possibility of expunging an earlier identity and reinventing herself: "I take the hint from the Ancient Mariner, who told his tale in order to be rid of it" (3). Coleridge's storyteller might tell his tale to the Wedding Guest in order to be rid of it, but he—like the reader—remains enthralled by it, destined to return again and again, with different audiences, to describe his fateful slaying of the albatross. Antin's zestful English prose betrays its origins and reinsinuates the past. In a transcendentalist affirmation of personal sovereignty, of the possibility of self-begetting, Antin concedes that our births are contingent events: "But once we are here, we may create our own world" (49). Yet a stubborn anterior world lurks behind every one of Antin's English words.

The implied reader of *The Promised Land* is Anglophonic exclusively, and the book comes equipped with a glossary to assist us in pronouncing and understanding the relatively few foreign terms—from Yiddish, Hebrew, Russian, and German—that Antin employs. The fact that such common words as *icon*, *ruble*, *Purim*, *vodka*, *Torah*, and *pogrom* are thought to require translation suggests how hermetically monolingual is the culture in which Antin, despite her study of both Latin and French in Boston schools, would now position herself. Multilingualism is a striking feature of the Polotzk that she would leave behind, not least by writing about that world in English. Antin notes the coexistence of varying amounts of Russian, Hebrew, and German with Yiddish in her native town. Within four months of her arrival in the United States, Antin is mastering English well enough that a school composition of hers, "Snow," is published in an education journal, sparking her ambition to be a writer, in English. Describing her loving acquisition of vocabulary in this new language unknown to Polotzk as "like gathering a posy blossom by blossom" (166), Antin reveals none of the anguish or regret that other translinguals have expressed. Joseph Conrad, for example, complained about the ordeal of writing in English, his third language, after Polish and French: "I had to work like a coal-miner in his pit quarrying all my English sentences out of a black night" (Letter 82). When Antin enrolls in a Chelsea public school in September 1894, she cannot even name the days of the week in English, yet she dismisses the enormous linguistic challenge she has to take on with the pronouncement that "I was Jew enough to have an aptitude for language in general, and to bend my mind earnestly to my task (*Land* 163). Of the Jewish language that she abjures, Yiddish, Antin says nothing.

Exulting in her triumphant self-reinvention as an Emersonian American, Antin marvels: "Over and over again I discover that I am a wonderful thing, am the repository of all the wisdom in the world, being alive and sane at the beginning of the twentieth century" (*Land* 197). Antin's hold on sanity is to prove more tenuous than she now realizes, but the most conspicuous evidence for the incompleteness of assimilation is provided by the author's father. A Talmudic scholar who has abandoned his calling and his faith, Pinchus Antin is ineffective at finding work to support his family. "But all told," his daughter tells us, "he did not earn enough to pay the rent in full and buy a bone for the soup" (*Land* 229). Nor is sister Frieda, reduced to drudgery to help pay household bills, a paragon of American accomplishment. However, aside from the straitened circumstances of the Antins at modest Crescent Beach, Chelsea, Wheeler Street, and Dover Street addresses, the most telling case for the unnaturalness of naturalization is Pinchus's failure at mastering the language of his new land, his inability ever to get beyond speaking an "impossible English" (161). Despite Mary's belief in a Jewish "aptitude for language in general," she attributes to her Jewish father "a natural inability to acquire the English language" and notes that, to the detriment of his ability to earn a living in Massachusetts, "he never learned to write correctly, and his pronunciation remains extremely foreign to this day" (161)—so claims his daughter, in fluent, if sometimes florid, English prose that testifies to her own apparent success at begetting herself anew as an Anglophonic American. "I have never had a dull hour in my life" (278), declares Antin implausibly, but dullness is deleted from the life she writes in English.

The numerous instances of successful translingualism that we have been studying should not inure us to the immensity of the achievement. Composing a book of literary merit in a language learned after childhood is a sufficiently daunting task that critics have questioned whether Jerzy Kosinski—who at the age of twenty-four arrived in the United States from Poland totally ignorant of English—could possibly have written the earliest books ascribed to him. In a scathing attack published in the *Village Voice* in 1982 and titled "Jerzy Kosinski's Tainted Words," Geoffrey Stokes and Eliot Fremont-Smith charged that the author probably wrote his first novel, *The Painted Bird* (1965), in Polish and then had it secretly translated by others into English. Hoffman, who departed Poland two years after Kosinski, in 1959, does not deny the ordeal of translingualism. Her own father, a cunning entrepreneur in Cracow but as feckless as Antin's in the ways of the New World, is less a counterpoint to Eva than a starker reminder of the incompleteness of all transformation. On the ship from Gdynia to Montreal, Hoffman resists the English lessons that another passenger offers. And when the family settles in Vancouver, she is distraught over how imperfectly the local language fits her universe: "the problem is that the signifier has become severed from the signified," she explains in the academic English she later mastered. "The words I learn now don't stand for things in the same way they did in my native tongue" (*Lost* 106).

Instead of the seamless transition from one language to another that Antin claims to have enjoyed, Hoffman finds herself suspended, inarticulately, between Polish and English: "Polish, in a short time, has atrophied, shriveled from sheer uselessness. Its words don't apply to my new experiences; they're not coeval with any of the objects, or faces, or the very air I breathe in the daytime. In English, words have not penetrated to those layers of my psyche from which a private conversation could proceed" (*Lost* 107). When they finally do penetrate, it occurs many years later as an epiphany in a classroom at the University of New Hampshire while Hoffman is teaching "The Love Song of J. Alfred Prufrock," the Eliot poem that is itself an ode to alienation but in whose contorted language she suddenly, ironically, feels at home. Whereas Antin's accomplished autobiography is testimony to her mastery of English, Hoffman's dwells on the tribulations and imperfections of translingualism. "Shuddup," Hoffman reports, is the first word she understands in English (*Lost* 104), a forbidding tongue that leaves the newcomer temporarily mute and permanently at a loss.

From its title to its final paragraph, in which Hoffman recites the recondite names of the flora in a Cambridge garden, *Lost in Translation: A Life in a New Language* problematizes its own medium and uses language as a metaphor for talking about the first four decades of a woman's life. "Like everybody," concludes Hoffman, "I am the sum of my languages—the language of my family and childhood, and education and friendship, and love, and the larger, changing world—though perhaps I tend to be more aware than most of the fractures between them, and of the building blocks" (273). That sum includes Antin's native Yiddish, though for Hoffman it is her parents' private code, "the language of money and secrets" (14). It also includes music, "the language of emotions" (70) that Hoffman learns to parse as a promising young pianist. In addition, it includes psychoanalysis, "the talking cure" that she samples as a rite of initiation into the American middle class, as well as the arcane semiotics of dating in Vancouver, which the adolescent Hoffman struggles to comprehend. But it is the problematic transition from Polish to English that constitutes the great drama of Hoffman's life and the central theme of her *Life in a New Language.*

Hoffman adduces the distinctive Polish *polot*—"a word that combines the meanings of dash, inspiration, and flying" (*Lost* 71)—and the peculiarities of the English *friend* (148) to argue that linguistic systems are not interchangeable. In effect endorsing the Sapir-Whorf thesis—the doctrine of linguistic determinism, which holds that each language is unique in the way it governs a speaker's apprehension of experience—Hoffman is aware that Polish enables certain thoughts and emotions she can never have in any other language and that English imposes perceptions and conceptions she might otherwise resist. "Nothing fully exists until it is articulated" (29), proclaims Hoffman—eager to enlarge her lexicon in English in order to endow the subtle variations among azaleas, hyacinths, forsythias, and delphiniums (280) with verbal habitation but also keenly aware that English and Polish cultivate different gardens. When, as a present for her fifteenth birthday, Hoffman is given a diary, her decision to construct a daily textual self in English rather than Polish is as momentous as Antin's early triumph at English composition. However, proceeding "as if the totality of the world and mind were coeval with the totality of language" (217), Hoffman lacks Antin's linguistic innocence. For Antin, achieving her dream of becoming an American means setting her agile mind to memorizing English vocabulary and then expunging Yiddish. But for Hoffman, translingualism leaves untidy traces.

Hoffman does experience moments of Antinesque exaltation, when the self seems lord of all it surveys, especially of that very self. "Perhaps we never know where we come from," she speculates; "in a way, we are all created ex nihilo" (23). But echoes of earlier identities belie the thought. Polish obtrudes through Hoffman's English, reminding her that languages are never exactly commensurate, that each always processes experience in its own unique way. *Lost in Translation* is suffused with the melancholy awareness that no single tongue suffices to digest the universe. Hoffman describes how, as a child, she once emitted a stream of nonsense syllables, sounds from a language beyond any language: "I want to tell A Story, Every Story, everything all at once, not anything in particular that might be said through the words I know, and I try to roll all sounds into one, to accumulate more and more syllables, as if they might make a Möbius strip of language in which everything, everything is contained. . . . I want articulation—but articulation that says the whole world at once" (11). As a translingual acutely aware of inhabiting the spaces between languages, Hoffman aspires to panlingualism, the potential of total expression not limited to the weltanschauung of any single system of expression. But she can enunciate her longings, she knows, only in one particular language at a time, and her English, unlike Antin's, is inflected with a mournful sense of its own inadequacy.

Yet Hoffman also nourishes a faint hope of redemption. Her book hints at conversion from the Whorfian view of a splintered post-Babel world to a Chomskyan belief in the Ur-language whose deep structures subsume any particular tongue: "Perhaps any language," she muses, "if pursued far enough, leads to exactly the same place" (274). Perhaps it ultimately does not matter whether one writes in English or in Polish, but Hoffman, in the here and now, recording her experiences in a persistent present tense, does not allow herself the luxury of ultimate thoughts.

Antin would have her readers believe that language is merely instrumental, a tool that can be adopted or discarded not only without trauma but also without distorting thought. But for Hoffman language is so fundamental and problematic that it serves as a metaphor for many of the other anxieties that she experiences. To describe the ineradicable gap between herself and her boyfriend at Rice, she explains: "my Texan and I know most poignantly that we don't speak exactly the same language" (190). Later, in Massachusetts, when she wants to describe how unintelligible her—unnamed—husband remains to her, Hoffman states that: "I still can't read the language of his feelings" (227). Her equivocations about whether to marry take the form of an interior dialogue, in English and Polish. Even psychoanalysis is presented as a linguistic activity: "For me, therapy is partly translation therapy, the talking cure a second-language cure" (271). And music, for which Hoffman evinces considerable talent, appeals to her precisely because it seems the consummate language: "Music is a wholly adequate language of the self—myself, everyone's self" (72).

Lost in Translation—whose title echoes Robert Frost's famous definition of poetry, a quality obliterated by the utter incompatibility of languages—closes in provisional reconciliation to its author's fallen state. If the world is constituted by language, then Hoffman's two concluding claims provide a soothing tautology: "The language of this is sufficient. I am here now" (280), she asserts in English prose, adequate for her purposes because for the moment it determines her purposes.

In saluting Antin as her "ancestress," a doppelgänger but for the fact that she was the creature of a different time, Hoffman recognizes the role of the Zeitgeist, in addition to language, in shaping purposes. If Hoffman had departed Europe in 1894 rather than 1959, she, too, likely would have spoken Yiddish instead of Polish. And if Antin had arrived in Boston in 1959, barely a decade after the extermination of most Yiddish speakers, she likely would not have been so nonchalant about renunciation of her *mama loshen*. A common history connects these two precocious women, but their autobiographies stand on either side of a vast historical divide. Whether or not, *pace* Adorno, it is possible to write poetry after Auschwitz, an eastern European Jew writes differently in the aftermath of the Holocaust. Though Antin was emphatically aware of anti-Semitism, including pogroms, she seems immune to bitterness or despair. But the specter of the Nazi death camps, which the author's parents barely managed to elude, haunts the prose of Hoffman's book. *The Promised Land* is a buoyant tale of faith fulfilled, while *Lost in Translation* is an ambiguous elegy for human sacrifice, not least of the author's childhood self.

Immigrants to America in the mid–twentieth century were confronted with a cultural landscape quite different from what those who arrived in 1894 had encountered. Individual identities are shaped by changing concepts of group identity. Though both Antin and Hoffman are uncomfortable with their designation as Jew, Antin—an enthusiastic convert to Americanism—writes before the category of "American Jewish literature" was reified and then ironized. Hoffman, by contrast, spurns both patriotism and tribalism. She suffers from a sense of belated arrival—in Poland, after the catastrophe, and in the United States, via Canada, after Saul Bellow, Bernard Malamud, and Philip Roth had already made it convenient to embrace—and possible to reject—the classification of American Jew.

Translingualism has been a consistent characteristic of Jewish culture in Babylon, Persia, Spain, Galicia, and other diasporas, as well as in the state of Israel, where only a plurality of the population is fully at home in Hebrew. But in North America in the second half of the twentieth century, the prospect, which Hoffman confronts, of life in a new language inspires fresh thoughts about language and about life.

7

BEGLEY JOINS THE FIRM

Priding herself on being a modern, New World atheist, young Mary Antin shocks her Chelsea classmates by announcing that she intends to attend school on the Passover holiday. Later she musters stoic valor when, having been invited by her teacher, Miss Dillingham, to visit her at home, she is served a slice of ham. Antin quietly violates the Jewish dietary taboo, but the ancient code of kashruth clearly exerts such residual power that as memoirist she recounts the episode in terms of epic deeds: "That Spartan boy who allowed the stolen fox hidden in his bosom to consume his vitals rather than be detected in the theft, showed no such miracle of self-control as did I, sitting there at my friend's tea-table, eating unjewish meat" (*Land* 197). For Eva Hoffman, Jewishness is important as an undesired burden, in the anti-Semitism that propels her family to emigrate from Cracow.

However, migration and translingualism do link Antin and Hoffman to Jewish history, to a people forced to wander through lands that echo with the sounds of alien tongues. Even before their dispersion, in A.D. 70, Hebrew speakers were often bilingual, with Greek, Latin, or Aramaic. However, it is a truism that, throughout the two thousand years of Diaspora, Jews cherished a portable text, the Torah, as if it were the real estate they were forbidden to possess. And the language of that text, Hebrew, was foregrounded and sacralized, studied and revered not as a semiotic instrument but as a hallowed object. Ceasing to be the medium of quotidian exchanges, it was reserved—and preserved—for pious communications. Every letter in its alphabet was scrutinized intently, as if it carried mystical import. And according to the system of *gematria*, in which letters signify numerical values and convey arcane messages, it did.

For practical transactions, Hebrew had to be supplemented by a secular language—another jargon peculiar to the Jews, such as Yiddish, Ladino, or Judeo-Arabic, and/or one of the Gentile languages of the ambient culture. "One language has never been enough for the Jewish people" (11), the critic Shmuel Niger observed in Yiddish, though he also wrote in Hebrew and Russian and though he also claimed that "A genuine writer has only one genuine language, just as he possesses only one self" (56). If so, then Jews have lacked genuine writers, since for most of their troubled history, knowledge of several languages has been a crucial survival mechanism; language has been crucial both to the survival of their distinctive culture and to their accommodation with the surrounding nations that threatened them. More so than for any other people, language has defined Jewish culture. And Jewish collective identity has been sustained through continued education and eloquence in distinctively Jewish languages and has thrived through the words of others' languages. Jewish literature is written in Hebrew, Yiddish, and Ladino; however, Jews have also excelled in Danish (Brandes, Goldschmidt), English (Bellow, Gordimer, Pinter); French (Montaigne, Proust, Jabès); German (Heine, Kafka, Celan); Hungarian (Molnár, Konrad); Italian (Levi, Svevo, Moravia); Polish (Schulz); Portuguese (Lispector, Scliar); Romanian (Manea); Russian (Mandelstam, Babel, Brodsky); Serbian (Kiš); and Spanish (Rojas, Gerchunoff). "From its inception," observed the Yiddish critic Ba'al-Makhshoves (pseudonym of Isidor Eliashev), "our literature has nearly always been a *bilingual* one" (75). And it has been bilingual, if not multilingual, not merely in the sense that two, three, or more languages formed the basis of the total polysystem by which Jewish culture functioned during any given era; but often the same authors expressed themselves in more than one language.

To the anti-Semite, Jewish linguistic versatility is not an asset but a symptom of pathology. In his infamous 1850 essay "Jewishness in Music," Richard Wagner insists that Jews can mimic but never really master the languages of the countries through which they pass: "The Jew speaks the language of the nation in whose midst he dwells from generation to generation, but he speaks it always as an alien. . . . In the first place, then, the general circumstance that the Jew talks the modern European languages merely as learned, and not as mother tongues, must necessarily debar him from all capability of therein expressing himself idiomatically, independently, and conformably to his nature" (51). According to the master of Bayreuth, language is a matter of birth, not acquisition, and since Heinrich Heine was born a Jew, German could never be his native language. If German was not his native language, he could never compose *echt* poetry in it. Wagner shares with W. B. Yeats, Thomas Jefferson, T. S. Eliot, Johann Wolfgang von Goethe, and George Santayana an aversion toward translingualism—a belief that the mother tongue is the only one that nurtures poetry, that "to make poetry in a foreign tongue has hitherto been impossible, even to geniuses of highest rank" (85). And since Wagner maintains that any language but Hebrew is forever alien to the Jew, the logical conclusion is that Jewish translinguals are condemned to be epigones not artists. According to the old guard of American academe, they could not even be professors, until Lionel Trilling finally received tenure at Columbia University in the 1930s. Though his native language was English, Trilling was told that it might be acceptable for an interloper to teach physics or biology, but it was inappropriate for a Jew to serve as steward of the English language.

Not everyone who examines the achievements of Jewish translinguals from ancient Aramaic to modern Esperanto (invented by the Jewish scholar Ludwig Zamenhof) will share the mistrust of Jewish translingualism. In medieval Spain, brilliant poets and commentators (for example, Yehuda Halevi, Solomon Ibn Gabirol, and Abraham Ibn Ezra) alternated between Hebrew and Arabic. In the nineteenth century, Yiddish and Hebrew competed for the attentions and affections of Jewish writers—often also with Russian, Polish, German, and other languages. Yiddish literature was almost entirely the creation of translinguals—individuals who adapted the jargon of the masses to literary purposes in order to try to reach these people as readers. Like Ngugi wa Thiong'o, turning from English to Gikuyu, or Kateb Yacine, from French to demotic Arabic, the pioneers of Yiddish literature deliberately chose a vernacular, working-class medium—at least for some of their writing. Yiddish was a part-time passion. "Of all nineteenth-century writers of consequence," observes Dan Miron, "only three wrote Yiddish from the start and never resorted to any other language for literary purposes" (7). Though they also wrote in the languages of eastern and central Europe, it was primarily Hebrew that served as the great partner and rival of Yiddish. The ambilingual Mendele Mokher Sforim declared that "for him writing in both Hebrew and Yiddish was like breathing through both his nostrils" (quoted in Miron 96). Employing a different metaphor to describe this literary translingualism, Ba'al-Makhshoves states that Jewish writers "live and breathe between two languages, even as a bridegroom is escorted to the bridal canopy by two parents" (72). But what is the language of the bride?

Hebrew ceased to be the language of mothers' lullabies throughout the long Diaspora. Could it again become the language of vital poetry? Modern Hebrew literature was created in the second half of the nineteenth century—just after the pioneering adaptation of Yiddish as a literary language—by an act of collective linguistic will. From the middle of that century until the creation of the State of Israel, when Hebrew began to be the first tongue of millions of citizens, aspiring Jewish authors turned to their ancient, dormant language after Yiddish, Polish, Russian, German, and other European languages. Shaul Tchernichowsky, who became one of the major poets in the new literature, had no acquaintance at all with Hebrew until the age of seven. And most of the others who invented modern Hebrew literature—including Yosef Chaim Brenner, Uri Zvi Greenberg, Uri Nissan Gnessin, Chaim Nachman Bialik, Abraham Shlonsky, S. Y. Agnon, and Achad Ha-Am—came to the language as their second, third, or fourth language and never entirely abandoned their others. In forging Hebrew into an instrument of modern expression, they had to contend with a paucity of vocabulary to deal with an urban, industrialized world and with a tradition of secular and realistic writing that was thinner than in the other languages they knew. But the early modern Hebrew authors chose their medium precisely in order to create such a tradition and to do so in a language that would affirm their identity within a vital and tenacious culture.

Louis Begley does not write in either Hebrew or Yiddish, but a transplant and a translingual, he is at the same time one of the most representative and extraordinary of Jewish authors currently publishing. For Begley and his characters, language is multiple and a mechanism of survival, through cunning adaptation. Born in Poland in 1933, Begley managed to live through the Holocaust—the single greatest challenge to Jewish continuity—in part through a linguistic glibness that enabled him to pass for Aryan. After the war, he began his life again in the United States and in English and then, in middle age, emerged in 1991 as an exceptional English-language author with the cunning truths of *Wartime Lies*.

For the novel's protagonist, nine-year-old Maciek, fluency in German is no academic matter. As a fugitive Galician Jew during the Nazi occupation of Poland, he does not attend school, but language offers him camouflage against those intent on exterminating all but Aryans. So, while careful to keep his identifying circumcision concealed from prying eyes, the boy masters the tongue of his tormentor by mimicking German broadcasts. He also ingratiates himself with a Gentile landlady, the widow of a Belgian engineer, by acquiescing to her desire to teach him French. However, perfect command of Polish is also crucial to eluding blackmailers who might threaten to betray a Jewish suspect to the police—"Although they often spoke themselves like true children of the slums, they could hear in the speech of a former eminent lawyer or professor of classics the unmistakable gay or sad little tune from the shtetl" (47).

In and through *Wartime Lies*, Louis Begley all but purged himself of those vulgar tunes. Published when its author was fifty-seven, this autobiographical first novel is a remarkably accomplished work of English prose. Though F. Scott Fitzgerald quipped that American lives have no second act, Begley, who moved to the United States in 1947, has managed to master a series of one-act roles. After eluding the Nazis through a variety of impersonations, Begley created a fresh, successful life for himself as head of the international-practice section of a prestigious New York law firm. In the consummate English sentences of the books he has thus far published, Begley reinvents himself again, late into middle age, as a master of translingual fiction. The eloquence of *Mistler's Exit* (1998), his fifth and latest volume, further disarms readers who might challenge an outsider's presumption. Begley has effectively forged identity papers as an important American author.

Wartime Lies begins with allusions to Virgil and Catullus and concludes with a melancholic Latin reminder of the mutability of names and ashes: "*Nomen et cineres una cum vanitate sepulta*" (181). The book—which quotes Dante in Italian, *Perché nostra colpa sì ne scipa?* (68), and an essential Jewish prayer in Hebrew, *Shema Yisrael* (71)—links language to lying and links lying to survival during the perilous time of war. Through elaborate deceits, Maciek, who calls himself Janek, passes for Catholic and thereby saves his own life. In the church he attends as cover, Maciek/Janek is taught that lying is a mortal sin, but his sacramental confessions disguise rather than disclose the truth. Narrated by the self-avowed false confessor himself, *Wartime Lies* is a book-length variation on the ancient Cretan paradox. When a liar concedes his mendacity, the reader is left with no standard of truth. Though the title *Wartime Lies* suggests a counterpoint to *Peacetime Truths*, we never discover what those verities are. After the Germans are routed, Poland remains a precarious place, and the narrator, who never does reveal his last name and remains "chained to the habit of lying" (156), continues to take Communion and to lie about himself even to his closest buddy, Koscielny. The implication is that every time is wartime and that control of language is always essential to survival.

If Begley the émigré storyteller is a tempered version of Maciek, so too is Ben, the titular character in Begley's second novel, *The Man Who Was Late* (1993)—a work of exquisite craft all the more impressive for the fact that its fastidious English is not the author's native tongue. *The Man Who Was Late* reenacts the prodigious rise and pathetic fall of Jay Gatsby (né James Gatz). Like *The Great Gatsby*, in which Nick Carraway tries to explain a deceased marvel of American social mobility, *The Man Who Was Late* is told to us by a friend of the eponymously tardy man, who is also late in the sense of deceased by the time the story is told. Jack is at home in America in a way that Ben, an immigrant Jew who came of age in plebeian Jersey City, could never have been. Whereas Ben fancies himself "his own invention" (35), Jack and his wife Prudence are the products of meticulous breeding through several generations of American gentry. Ben is a bounder, but despite Jack's "well-bred prejudice against strivers and achievers" (18), Jack is fascinated by Ben's facility in making himself over, in assimilating the details of dressing and dining precisely comme il faut. A science writer for a magazine with generous deadlines, Jack is a connoisseur of long lunches and estimably nebulous subjects—like precolonial Indians of Maine. But then, as Ben's heir and executor, Jack becomes almost vulgarly zealous in trying to piece together an understanding of his late friend.

After Harvard and a finishing stint in the marines, Ben is hired as the "house Jew" for "a Wall Street investment bank that was both powerful and impeccably elegant" (7). He builds a splendid career upon deft deceptions. Ben is as resourceful as the urchin Maciek, except that his theater is no longer the mean streets of Warsaw or the potato fields of rural Poland but the globe. And Ben, too, appropriates languages—English, French, Portuguese, Japanese—to ingratiate himself with the financial rulers of the world. Wartime has been succeeded by an era of international business, yet another occasion for self-sustaining lies. When his marriage to Rachel, a wealthy widow with twin daughters, disintegrates, Ben moves to Paris to head his firm's continental operations and continue to refine himself into a paragon of epicurean grace. There, Ben meets Jack's married Gallic cousin, Véronique. Smitten with each other, they conduct a torrid love affair until Véronique's feckless husband, Paul, finds out. She publicly casts her lot with Ben, but he flees the camp of commitment and heads out for Brazil and Japan, where a marathon of business meetings and costly dissipations almost diverts him from thoughts of Véronique.

"Always when he found himself in a strange city, Ben skimmed the pages of the telephone directory, looking for his own name and other surprises" (150). In a lucid Rio de Janeiro dawn, after reading an account in *O Globo* of ceremonies to commemorate the Warsaw ghetto, Ben stalks the local directory for traces of his abandoned past: "The Rio book listed many Jewish names, extravagantly spelled. Feinbaum from Galicia had become Vainboim. Others retained special, Polish transliterations: Bernsztajn instead of the banal Bernstein; Grynszpan, Lakman, Szpigel, others" (150). However, for all his stops in strange cities, for all the telephone directories he must have scanned, we never learn whether Ben encounters "his own name and other surprises"—for the simple reason that we never learn his family name, just as Maciek never reveals his. Ben is simply, defiantly Ben. Ben the international banking maven has begotten himself with a cosmopolitan identity purged of ethnic encumbrances. Jack and his fellow patricians are impressed: "They agreed that Ben's was a virtuoso performance" (222).

And yet Ben is keenly aware of the flaw in his performance—of how, despite all his studied nonchalance, "He was late and would never catch up" (16) with people like Jack and Rachel, who seem to a Polish refugee to have been born with a patina of natural polish. It is as though Wagner was right all along: Jewish translingualism will always be a fraud. "I have thrown away a pearl richer than all my tribe" (221), Ben laments, echoing Othello and faulting himself for squandering the love of Véronique. And he never quite succeeds in purging himself of traces of his tribe, a slaughtered people never more assertive than in their annihilation. Swimming far from shore at Copacabana, Ben feels a recurrence of his ancient "tropism toward death" (161), and he embraces the powerful currents that are pulling him away from safety. Later, Ben is drawn to a Nazi named Dr. Willi, a Teutonic dentist who doubles as a Rio pimp and helps the lonely Jew abandon himself to sensual distraction.

Ben is a magnificent survivor, a man who remakes himself in accordance with his own idea of poise. But he is as hopelessly extinct as Jack's precolonial Indians. *The Man Who Was Late* recounts the life-and-death struggle of an extraordinary figure who seeks to court both life and death as methodically as he conquers a woman, Véronique. If, ultimately, Ben's tropism toward death overcomes his command of life, it is because he is a man who is late even before his demise. He has adopted extinction as a tactic of endurance. Jack adopts Ben, posthumously, as a literary subject, though the only work of imagination that Jack has ever published is a short novel loosely based on the drowning of his older brother Sam, a war hero. Left to ponder Ben's notes and letters, Jack determines to undertake a second short book, the story of another drowned brother—a further, belated casualty of unresolved conflict. It will be the second Begley novel, another account of wartime lies, in which forging an identity is desperate combat and fraught with fraud.

Unlike Maciek and Ben, Maximilian "Max" Hafter Strong, the

narrator of Begley's third novel, *As Max Saw It* (1994), is a native of the United States and not much of a picaro, not nearly as alert as the others to the main or even minor chance. *As Max Saw It* is a powerful novel about AIDS, made all the more powerful by the fact that its obtuse narrator never mentions the dreaded disease. Mortifying the emotions, refusing to allow themselves to be overwhelmed by loss, fortifies both Maciek and Ben. And emotional insulation protects and mocks Max Strong's strength.

"I am curious about obligations" (9), declares Max, by way of explaining why he teaches contract law at Harvard University. A curiosity about obligations is obligatory for any reader who would profit from *As Max Saw It*, the professor's fictional memoir of an unlikely friendship. However, Max, who writes an acclaimed treatise on contracts, demonstrates his curiosity through distance, through strategies of evasion. Though he admits that "Relationships did not stick to me," *As Max Saw It* is a meditation on relationships and obligations that the law professor has, willy-nilly, accumulated over the course of sixteen years and more. They continue to cling, whether or not Max acknowledges their claims on his memory and imagination. It is unlikely that readers will view the experience that Begley's narrator recounts quite as Max saw it.

As Max Saw It begins on the day that the narrator and Arthur, an old college chum, arrive at La Rumorosa, a sumptuous villa on the shores of Lake Como that is owned by Edna Joyce, another acquaintance from their days as Harvard undergraduates. Arthur is an opportunistic businessman who has cultivated the art of sponging off the rich, and Max, an obscure professor accustomed to living as and with a graduate student, is touring Europe by tagging along. The novel concentrates closely on the private lives of privileged characters, men and women with enough assets to indulge sumptuous tastes in dining, housing, and travel. Like *The Man Who Was Late*, Begley's work shows a fine eye for the ranks and perquisites of wealth, an outsider's avidity for and arrogation of the totems of entitlement. However, brief allusions to public events—Richard Nixon's resignation, the Tiananmen Square massacre, John Hinckley's assault on Ronald Reagan, the death of Baseball Commissioner Bart Giamatti, the fall of the Berlin Wall—calibrate the time frame and remind us that no one, neither

Nixon nor Max, can extricate himself entirely from history. Withdrawal into the merely personal is as futile as expecting immunity from a plague, especially during the age of AIDS.

At La Rumorosa, Max is immediately implicated in the life of Charlie Swan, another Harvard classmate though four years Max's senior. In Cambridge, tall, brash Charlie was "noted for his prowess in a single scull and with a martini shaker" (4), but he has since become an internationally renowned architect. Though they have not seen each other for more than ten years, Charlie greets Max bluntly, favoring him with intimate confidences, as though recognizing in the reserved professor some mystic link to his own effusive self. While Charlie and all the other house guests spend the morning touring the region around La Rumorosa, Max stays behind and encounters by the poolside an extraordinarily attractive sixteen-year-old youth whom he describes as "Eros himself, longhaired and dimpled, his skin the color of pale amber" (12). He is Toby, Charlie's protégé and an apprentice in his Geneva office. A few years later, while in Beijing to advise the Chinese government on legal matters, Max runs into Charlie and Toby again and discovers that they are lovers.

In passing, Max, who comes of undistinguished Rhode Island stock, reveals a few details about his own life. He has inherited great wealth from a cousin in Pennsylvania, and he has married an Englishwoman, Camilla, who works at Harvard's Fogg Museum. But the narrator's own fortunes are made to seem incidental to the story of Charlie and Toby and how it intersects with Max's story. The professor's newly acquired riches enable him to purchase a rural retreat in the Berkshires, near one built by Charlie. Max and Camilla spend long weekends and vacations away from Cambridge in the company of Charlie and Toby as well as other unusual figures—including Edwina and Ricky Howe, dotty English aristocrats who rotate residences to avoid taxes, and Roland Cartwright, a raffish English documentarian whom Max suspects of sleeping with Camilla. When Camilla announces that she is returning alone to London to accept a position at the National Gallery, Max is too detached from his own relationships to react in any way except fall sleep.

More notable to Max than the disintegration of his marriage is the relationship between Charlie and Toby that, despite disparities of age and social status, endures to Charlie's sixtieth birthday. On the evening of the celebration, it becomes indubitably clear that Toby, who has developed sores on his face, hands, and forearms, is gravely ill. A few months later, he dies in severe pain and in Charlie's bed.

Out of what he characterizes as "a mixture of respect for Toby's dignity, squeamishness about illness, and fear of reaching that point where pity intersects with contempt" (125), Max restrains his curiosity about his friend's dire condition. The death itself occurs as if offstage; we jump abruptly from a sickbed conversation between Toby and Max to Toby's snowy funeral. It is only later, indirectly, that we learn something of Toby's final moments, when Max recounts a memory that Charlie shared. It is apparent from his symptoms that Toby dies of AIDS, the lethal, epidemic disorder that has disproportionately afflicted homosexual men. However, *As Max Saw It* is an AIDS novel that never once mentions the awful acronym. At least two of its three chief characters are gay, yet although Charlie in conversation with Max delights in flouting prim conventions, the narrator is remarkably reticent about men's love for other men. At one point, Charlie teases Max with the suggestion that he himself might not mind being seduced by Toby. Though later admitting that "I was moved by his beauty" (101), Max never responds explicitly to Charlie's suggestion. Is he merely repressing his homosexual inclinations? If so, is such repression a manifestation of anxiety and obsession? Max professes all-consuming love for Laura, the Italian art dealer whom he marries after lawyerly, long-distance correspondence, yet his text is much more attentive to Toby than to Laura. In its final pages, his joy in Laura's pregnancy is overshadowed by his shock at Toby's death. While Max does not explicitly subscribe to Charlie's blatantly misogynous definition of woman—"a hole filled with juice that starts to smell like fish upon contact with air" (52)—his memoir is partial to its male characters.

After divorcing Camilla, Max learns that his first wife had been unfaithful to him—though not with Roland but with Toby. The implications of that fact are astounding, but aside from a temporary pique over betrayed friendship, Max—ever the judicious, prudent scholar of jurisprudence—never acknowledges astonishment or even any awareness of the possibilities. Since the AIDS virus is most commonly transmitted through sexual contact, it is quite possible that Toby infected Camilla, who in turn infected Max. Readers are left to ponder the likelihood that their narrator is dying of the same harrowing disease that killed Toby; Max does no such pondering himself.

He does inform us that he donated blood for a transfusion during Toby's final days. "I am glad that they are going to fill me up with your blood," says Toby; "Charlie also has the same type, so our three bloods are getting all mixed up together" (130). Max merely records the proclamation of fraternity without any commentary other than an eavesdropping nurse's observation: "We're all related like that . . . only people don't take time to think about it" (130). Preoccupied with abstract concepts of contract law, Max either does not take the time to think about his fellowship with Charlie and Toby or else refuses to concede it to the reader or to himself.

Max's most dramatic act of denial occurs in the concluding paragraphs of the novel, which record Charlie's account of the architect's final moments with Toby. Charlie recalls how, distraught over the agony and impending death of his lover, he rushed into the bathroom and cut up his own cheeks and gums until the blood flowed freely. He then returned to Toby in bed and brought him to orgasm. Since the most efficient way of transmitting the AIDS virus is sexually and through an open, bloody wound, Charlie's action cannot but be seen as a kind of desperate Liebestod, a romantic suicide. Max gives no indication that this is the way he sees it or that he realizes that, infected through Camilla with Toby's AIDS, his blood flows with the same fatal virus inhabiting both Charlie and Toby.

Max visits China, as a coddled official guest, twice during the sixteen years covered by the novel. He is more comfortable as an outsider in Beijing, behaving according to a formal code of manners, than as an intimate in Massachusetts, where the etiquette seems more confused. He revels in his role as benefactor to Wang Jun Jun, an attractive Chinese guide, but after she comes to study at Harvard, he detaches himself from her when their relationship threatens to undermine his defensive routines. Max is appointed Elijah Wooden Professor of Jurisprudence at Harvard—a title that, Camilla teases, "fits him to a T" (85). Charlie Swan, whose parents christened him in sly tribute to the Proustian character who wastes his life in quest of an unattainable and unworthy love, asks Max: "Do you believe in the fatal irony of names?" (64). Maximilian Hafter Strong lacks the strength of character to confront the multiple ironies that are so evident to a reader. A wooden, prudent scholar, he is an incongruous choice to narrate a tale of fatal passion that defies convention.

Immaculately spare and controlled, outlander Begley's hard-won English style recalls the delicate finesse of Henry James. But a more obvious precedent for *As Max Saw It* might be *The Good Soldier*, the 1915 novel that Ford Madox Ford subtitled *A Tale of Passion*—though Dowell, its narrator, an emotional eunuch oblivious to the lurid events he is reporting, is ill-equipped to talk of passion. Read obliquely, across what Max concedes having seen, Begley's text admits a rich range of emotions and experiences. Beyond Max's measured cadences, in the cosmic wartime that the professor's lies deny, we can hear a wilder strain, the macabre music of the spheres that Charlie identifies as "the upgathered howl of pain, rising from every corner of the earth. Like a toilet bowl that has overflowed and yet some idiot keeps flushing" (141). Charlie's sanitational simile renders *As Max Saw It* veritably Shakespearean in its intimations of a universal void. For all Max's bonhomie, his is a tale told by an idiot.

In contrast to the denials, effacements, and replacements of self that shape Begley's first three books, stories in which language conceals as much as reveals, his fourth novel tells us quite a bit about Schmidt: That he is a prosperous, sixty-year-old lawyer recently widowed and recently retired. That, after selling the Fifth Avenue apartment he and Mary, a book editor, kept as their New York base, he occupies the splendid Bridgehampton house at which they spent weekends and summers. That, for all his worldly success, he confesses to a friend: "I am lonely and lost" (75). That he considers his only child, Charlotte, who handles public relations for a tobacco company, "a smug, overworked yuppie" (73). That, though Schmidt sponsored her fiancé in his own illustrious law firm and even introduced him to Charlotte, he resents Jon Riker as "a wonk, a turkey, a Jew!" (13). That, though Jon and

Charlotte have lived together for four years, Schmidt resists their plans to marry. *About Schmidt* is another Begley take on bounding, this time from inside the boundary looking out.

Interrogating himself, Albert Schmidt, aka Schmidtie, ponders whether decent behavior is adequate to demonstrate virtue and whether self-scrutiny is sufficient for self-awareness. To be sure, Schmidtie's best friend, successful movie director Gil Blackman, is Jewish, but the prospect of his own daughter's joining the tribe, through marriage and conversion, irks. So do senescence, solitude, and a reduction in his pension. Schmidt is a specialist in bankruptcy litigation, and his own spiritual divestiture is a comic turn on *King Lear*.

If you want to learn about Schmidt, you can start with genteel bigotry, but *About Schmidt* is the stinging account of a venomless WASP who counts himself a lion in winter. In the arms of Carrie, a Puerto Rican waitress less than half his age who might herself be half-Jewish, and in the clutches of her boorish boyfriend Bryan, Schmidtie is both a lion and a pigeon. "Could he not sail alone beyond the pillars of Hercules and taste the apples of the western garden before the waves closed over his head?" (60), asks Schmidtie, echoing Tennyson's Ulysses. Like the aging Greek hero, the protagonist of Begley's fourth novel is not yet ready to renounce adventure. Exquisitely droll sentences navigate a subtle passage between the Scylla of pluck and the Charybdis of pathos. Parsing out the tax consequences of bestowing the house in Bridgehampton on the newlyweds, Schmidtie is a hybrid of largesse and finesse—like Shakespeare's Jewish Shylock, equally attentive to his daughter and his ducats.

Schmidt regards Renata Riker, a psychiatrist and the mother of his prospective son-in-law, as "the Sphinx in the Sahara of my affections" (147). Encounters between the two are a wry duel of fine minds honed on Blackstone and Freud, respectively. Begley the international corporate lawyer manages to make hassles over codicils compelling. A Holocaust survivor, he makes illuminating light of the gloom of anti-Semitism.

As though it were a truth universally acknowledged that a sixty-year-old widower in possession of a good fortune must be in want of a twenty-year-old mistress, Schmidtie succumbs to the charms of the cunning pauper Carrie, as thoroughly as Maciek manages to beguile his lethal foes. The epigraph from *Don Giovanni* with which *About Schmidt* begins—"Già che spendo i miei danari, / Io mi voglio divertir"—is rendered in the original Italian, but Schmidt, whose emotional armor is almost as rigid as Max's, lacks the resiliency to be as polyglot as Maciek or Ben. Instead, it is the upstarts who are linguistic nomads—the Hispanic Carrie and the Francophonic Vietnamese servant with whom Schmidtie endangered his marriage. Though he can intone a few operatic arias, Schmidtie—who even finds speaking honest English as difficult as "using the one foreign language he had learned and forgotten, his high school French"—is obdurately monolingual. Begley, by contrast, repeats the translingual triumph of Joseph Conrad, offering homage to the earlier Polish master by having Schmidtie read *Nostromo* on a beach in Manaus. He spends a brief, solitary vacation there distracted and mute.

The fact that Schmidt dines regularly at a local Bridgehampton restaurant named O'Henry's should alert the reader to a reversal of fortune on the final page. But it is the richer legacy of Jane Austen, Henry James, and Edith Wharton to which Begley—who emerged from cultural margins to the presidency of PEN American Center in 1994—lays claim, again, in superbly nuanced English prose. However much those analysts of refined sensibilities might have resented the upstart immigrant Jew, he has become a partner in the firm.

As senior partner in a prosperous advertising firm, Thomas Hooker Mistler III, the eponymous protagonist of Begley's latest novel, revels in economic power and wallows in regret. At the outset of *Mistler's Exit*, he is diagnosed with terminal cancer of the liver but decides to forgo futile treatment. Pretending it is a business trip, Mistler travels alone to Venice, intent on spending "a paltry ten days of serene emptiness" (18). But memory and desire intrude. So do a younger woman, Lina Verano, who shows up in his hotel bedroom, and a woman of his own advanced middle age, Bunny Cutler, who might have been the love of his life, if he had lived it differently. *Mistler's Exit*, which makes sly allusion to Ezra Pound, Igor Stravinsky, Sergey Diaghilev, and Gustav von Aschenbach, rewrites Thomas Mann's *Death in Venice*, in English, as the valediction of an accomplished American executive haunted by what has and might have been.

The novel begins in French, with a cynical epigraph from Jacques Chardonne's 1964 *Demi-jour*: Death means no great loss because we never know what we lose, and all's well that merely ends—"*Ce que les hommes vont perdre, tant pis; ils ne s'en apercevront pas. Tout finit bien puisque tout finit.*" But despite several French and Italian phrases scattered throughout the text, Begley tells his tale in spare, immaculate English, with an eye for precisely the right phrase and an ear for the proper rhythms of Anglophonic prose. "You look and sound like an Englishman" (204), says a stranger to Mistler, an American in Venice whose author has mastered his acquired language as if he were to the grammar born. His son Sam even teaches at Stanford University, in the Department of English.

It is hard to imagine a character more remote from Maciek, the little Jewish magpie who borrows the ambient language in order to survive in wartime Poland. Born "with a silver spoon stuck firmly in his mouth" (8), Mistler has always been a member of the American plutocracy, at ease in standard English and in a limousine. He does admit to having one Jewish great-grandmother, but that arcane information only serves to emphasize how thoroughly Protestant, English, and patrician his Yankee bloodlines otherwise are. Yet in imagining Mistler's exit, Begley is merely reconfiguring the terms of Maciek's entrance. What Mistler shares with Maciek—as well as Begley's other protagonists Ben, Max, and Schmidt—is a genius for self-invention and self-deception. Despite being heir to a prosperous family business—a venerable Wall Street investment bank—and a sumptuous legacy, Mistler privately regards himself as a self-made man, if only because he braved his father's disdain to found his own advertising agency. Making of himself a legend in the field, he overcame fierce competition by devising wartime lies, dissembling to his associates, his rivals, his wife, his son, and himself.

While still at Harvard, Mistler, we are told, harbored longings to write the great American novel, and he later convinced himself that his advertising work was just a daytime job, designed to endow him with respectability while he scribbled away at night. At twenty-nine, Mistler published his first novel, a book that made little impact and that he himself conceded "lacked both ambition and vigor" (12). There was no second novel, and the advertising business, which he thought of as a mere avocation, monopolized Mistler's creative energies. Despite his pretensions of being a self-made man, Mistler resists responsibility for the course of his career even as the prospect of his death concentrates his mind. "Fate had not condemned him to eat his heart out writing" (12) is the way he rationalizes his abandonment of literary aspirations. Yet fate had put a fortune at his disposal, and he need not have starved in a garret while courting the Muse. If Mistler did not become a novelist, it was, like the fact that he did not become Bunny Cutler's lover at Harvard, because of choices that he made but refused to acknowledge.

Mistler notes that his image is missing from his family photographs, "for the very good reason that normally he took them" (21). In an important sense, the real Mistler—another version of the man who was late—is also missing from his own life, for the reason that he is the one who has fabricated that life in a way that conceals the identity of its author from the other characters, from the reader, and from himself. Dying in Venice, Mistler is astute about furniture, clothing, and wine but still lacking in self-awareness. The way he—as well as Max, Maciek, Ben, and Schmidt—saw it is not the way that the reader does.

The five family photographs—*Wartime Lies*, *As Max Saw It*, *About Schmidt The Man Who Was Late*, and *Mistler's Exit*—that Begley has thus far offered up for view all focus on characters who construct and falsify themselves. In and through each, an extraordinary translingual author makes himself invisible and ubiquitous.

8

SAYLES GOES SPANISH

Throughout *To Be or Not to Be* (1942), Ernst Lubitsch's mordant mockery of Nazi aggression against Poland, Jack Benny and Carole Lombard, playing married actors in a Warsaw theater troupe, speak fluent American English. In the 1983 remake, Mel Brooks and Anne Bancroft, reprising the Benny and Lombard parts, begin the proceedings prattling in Polish. However, several minutes into the film, a disembodied, Olympian voice announces: "Ladies and gentlemen, in the interests of sanity and clarity, the rest of this movie will *not* be in Polish." And Brooks and Bancroft immediately resume conjugal squabbling, in English. One of the protocols of commercial movie production is that characters such as Oskar Schindler, Christopher Columbus, Eva Perón, and Jesus are really speaking something else when what we hear from the actor's mouth is Queen's—or Queens—English. Tony Curtis's portrayal in *Spartacus* of a Roman slave with a Bronx inflection is legendary. The convention of cinematic monolingualism obviates the clumsy mechanisms of subtitles and dubbing, even as it reinforces a popular belief that all the world speaks English, only and always.

Reverence for convention is not a conspicuous feature of films by John Sayles, one of the few authentically independent *auteurs* successful in getting his work produced, marketed, and distributed within a system controlled by conglomerates. Sayles has written and edited most of the twelve works he has also directed, and most are an exercise in negative capability, a leap of sympathetic imagination into a world quite different from his own—white, middle-class, male, heterosexual, and Anglophonic. In *Lianna* (1983), Sayles focuses on the life of a lesbian. In *The Brother from Another Planet* (1984), the protagonist is not only an alien—to the United States as well as to the Earth—but his skin is dark, and he finds a home in Harlem. To make *Matewan* (1987), Sayles projected himself into the struggles of West Virginia coal miners during the 1920s. With *City of Hope* (1990), the setting is a squalid urban jungle. With *Limbo* (1999), it is the southeastern coast of Alaska. With *Lone Star*, which won an Imagen Award as the 1996 feature that best portrayed Latinos, Sayles moved to fictional Rio County, Texas, along the border with Mexico. His next film strays well beyond that border and beyond the realm of Anglophonia. *Hombres Armados / Men With Guns* is a daring case of cinematic translingualism in which the filmmaker leaps past the barriers of language. Though he is an Anglo from Hoboken, New Jersey, Sayles made his eleventh movie in Spanish.

Literary history abounds with what Ilan Stavans calls "tongue snatchers" (204), writers, including S. Y. Agnon, Chinua Achebe, Samuel Beckett, Paul Celan, Joseph Conrad, Isak Dinesen, Vladimir Nabokov, R. K. Narayan, Fernando Pessoa, and Léopold Senghor, who have distinguished themselves in an adopted language. And a director who abandons the native tongue as artistic medium is not exactly unprecedented. Since books are made of words and movies are made of images, translingualism is less arduous for a filmmaker than for a poet. Yet Ingmar Bergman's sole excursion into English, *The Touch* (1972), is not among his masterpieces, and when, in the same year, Michelangelo Antonioni attempted to capture the American counterculture through California English, the result, *Zabriskie Point*, was a fiasco. However, Hollywood owes much of its glory to what xenophonic émigrés such as Michael Curtiz, Fritz Lang, Ernst Lubitsch, Rouben Mamoulian, Douglas Sirk, Josef von Sternberg, Billy Wilder, and Fred Zinnemann were able to accomplish with screenplays in English. And recent American cinema has continued to recruit translingual directors, including Ang Lee, Constantin Costa-Gavras, Roland Emmerich, Milos Forman, Agniezska Holland, Louis Malle, Wolfgang Petersen, Paul Verhoeven, and John Woo.

Directors from throughout the hemisphere who have in recent years moved from native Spanish into global English include Alfonso Arau, Guillermo Del Toro, Luis Mandoki, and Luis Puenzo. But when they—or authors such as Felipe Alfau, Ariel Dorfman, Rosario Ferré, Alberto Manguel, Manuel Puig, and Ilan Stavans—stray into English from Spanish for one work or more, it is not quite the same as what Sayles has done. Julia Alvarez recounted in supple, acquired English the story of immigrant Dominican assimilation into the dominant Yankee culture in *How the García Girls Lost Their Accents*. However, Sayles taught himself Spanish in order to move to the margins, to represent experiences rarely given words in Hollywood. "All my mother does is work," says Pilar Cruz (Elizabeth Peña) in *Lone Star*. "That's how you get to be Spanish." Sayles claims that he got to speak Spanish by working at it on his own less than a decade earlier. Sayles's working proficiency in the language is testimony to a stubborn determination to portray life as it is lived beyond the syntactical structures of his imperial native tongue. If, as Wittgenstein asserted, the limits of one's language are the limits of one's world, Sayles refuses to confine himself to one language, even to the capacious territory to which the *Oxford English Dictionary* holds title.

Sayles's transition to Spanish was already apparent in the remarkable novel he published in 1991: *Los Gusanos*, a fiction set in Miami and Cuba that immerses its reader in the lives of disparate characters—revolutionaries, counterrevolutionaries, CIA agents, drug lords, peasants, professors, merchants, old, young, male, female, brown, black, and white—likely to be as alien to the reader as to their author. And most are likely to be speaking the *lengua* that Sayles places upon their tongues. A story of the émigrés Castro castigated as "worms," *Los Gusanos* is one of the most compelling Cuban novels ever written from the mainland, and its authority is enhanced by the fact that, though the narration itself is in English, most of the dialogue is in (untranslated but decipherable) Spanish. From its title to a parting "*Que pasò?*" on the final page, Sayles created a novel that, *pace* Whorf, dissects nature along lines not uttered in English. It is fidelity to his characters that likewise determined the language in which Rolando Hinojosa-Smith wrote each volume of his Klail City cycle, a multigenerational narrative set in the Rio Grande valley. For earlier characters, the dialogue—as well as the narration—is in Spanish, while later developments in the story are told, as they would be lived, in English. Though he lacks the Chicano's linguistic advantages, Sayles shares a commitment to verbal authenticity.

So, with a little help from Mexican writer Alejandro Springall—"translating my bad Spanish into better Spanish" (Sayles, Interview)—Sayles wrote *Hombres Armados / Men with Guns*, a movie set in an unnamed, generic Latin American country, in the language that his characters would be speaking. Nor, he explained in the production notes distributed by Sony Pictures, did he wish to impose an additional burden on the largely Latin American cast: "It made no sense for me to have the actors struggling with their English, or doing their scenes phonetically, rather than concentrating on their acting." With the notable exception of Polish cinematographer Slawomir Idziak, most of the crew spoke Spanish. Shooting in Chiapas, Mexico City, and Veracruz, Sayles managed to run the set *en español*: "Sometimes I had a problem if two or three people were talking at the same time. I'd have to ask them to slow down," he states in the production notes.

The first sounds—like the last sounds—we hear in *Hombres Armados* are, in fact, not Spanish but the twittering of birds, an exquisite avian song that mocks the words of men with guns. Then we hear a peasant woman addressing her young daughter in Kuna, a language spoken exclusively on a single island off the coast of Panama. Along with Nahuatl, Tzotzil, and Maya, it is one of several non-European languages spoken by the rural Indians during Dr. Humberto Fuentes's journey away from the city and into the mountains. The final words of the film are also spoken in Kuna. As much as the North American viewer, Fuentes (Federico Luppi), a seasoned physician whose practice is limited to the affluent in his country's capital, travels into an alien landscape where Spanish sometimes *no se habla*. For years, as part of an international health-services program, he has been preparing young volunteers to treat the sick in indigent indigenous villages. Recently widowed, Fuentes decides to take a vacation in the mountains and visit his former students on the job. It has been three years since he has had contact with any of them.

It is as imprudent a plan as if he had intended to tour the synagogues of Vienna in 1938. Everyone else seems keenly aware that the national army and a guerrilla insurgency are bloodying the ground precisely where Fuentes aims to go. One of his patients, an army general, tries but fails to dissuade him from taking his trip. "You're like a child, Humberto," declares the military officer; "The world is a savage place." Though Fuentes is oblivious, the viewer can infer that his eminent patient contributes to the savagery. And

Bravo (Roberto Sosa)—a former student, now reduced to dealing drugs, whom the doctor tracks down in the squalid neighborhood called Los Perdidos—is exasperated by Fuentes's naïveté. "You're the most learned man I ever met," Bravo tells his old teacher, "but also the most ignorant."

The movie's credits acknowledge that "The character of Dr. Fuentes was inspired by the character of Dr. Arrau who appears in the novel *The Long Night of White Chickens* by Francisco Goldman." However, Fuentes's pedigree can be traced back even further than the 1993 fiction, written in English by the Guatemalan-American author and set in the Guatemalan civil war. Suffering from a heart condition that makes him look a bit like the Knight of Mournful Countenance, the recently widowed, white-haired doctor sallies forth on his quest alone—ethereal Don Quixote, without the earthy grounding of Sancho Panza. Instead of Rocinante, he relies on a Jeep sports utility vehicle. Asked once to name his twenty favorite political films, Sayles listed Nikita Mikhalkov's *Burnt by the Sun* (1994), which he described as "A lament for the loss of idealism." *Hombres Armados* is another such lament, and its star—and starry—idealist is a doctor who still believes in immortality through altruism. "Every man should have a legacy," insists Fuentes, but he soon discovers that his has been expunged. He had hoped to make a lasting contribution to his country by preparing a younger generation of doctors to serve the rural poor. But each of the eager physicians he has trained to propagate among the peasantry the benefactions of modern medicine has disappeared, an innocent victim of brutal men with guns.

Fuentes is implausibly oblivious to the dangers he is courting, but convincing the doctor to get out on the road seems more important to Sayles than convincing the viewer that the doctor would do it. The terrain through which he wanders is on the map of myth, inaccessible by ordinary transportation. Fuentes passes through areas identified, successively, with the Salt People, Sugar People, Coffee People, Banana People, Gum People, Corn People, and Sky People. "Creo únicamente en progreso" [I believe only in progress], proclaims the gentle doctor, confident in the power of science to advance humankind. However, his pilgrim's progress across the killing fields of Latin America is a lesson in human cruelty. Fuentes eventually concedes that "El mundo es durissimo" [the world is a very hard place], on the basis of abundant evidence. Sayles positions his traveling allegory somewhere south of Mexico, though if it were not for the languages his characters speak, the location could be Bosnia, Rwanda, Afghanistan, Sri Lanka, East Timor, or anywhere else that human life is prey to men with guns.

During the course of his symbolic journey into the heart of darkness—nearly a century after Mr. Kurtz, Joseph Conrad's evangelist of European enlightenment, was found dying in the African bush—Dr. Fuentes acquires archetypal companions. The first to attach himself to the traveler is Conejo (Dan Rivera González), an urchin, the fruit of rape, who has been fending for himself after rejection by his mother. Casual about the horrors he has witnessed in the mountains, the foul-mouthed boy Conejo is as cynical as the fatherly Fuentes is sanguine. The child helps guide the man through a rugged region for which his maps have not prepared him.

Also acting as Fuentes's guide is Domingo (Damián Delgado), a deserter from the army who is haunted, in garishly lit flashbacks, by guilt over atrocities he committed while in uniform. Domingo joins the motley troupe of travelers after pointing his (unloaded) gun at Fuentes and Conejo and relieving them of their cash. After Fuentes treats the gunshot wound that Domingo later receives, the bitter renegade eventually is healed. "I wanted to leave something in the world," laments Fuentes, who despairs after each of his medical students vanishes in the bloody field. However, it is Domingo—a former medic who concludes the film by agreeing to treat a peasant woman injured by an army mine—who will be the failing doctor's spiritual heir.

Another comrade whom Fuentes, like Dorothy on the road to Oz, picks up along the way is Padre Portillo (Damián Alcázar), a gentle Catholic priest who has lost both his faith and his calling. In one of the most striking sequences in *Hombres Armados*, Portillo recounts, with the aid of flashbacks, the spiritual crisis that shattered his confidence in his sacred vocation: "I was tested, and I was weak." The ordeal occurred in an Indian village that was delivered this ultimatum from an army *commandante*: Either execute six suspected subversives among you who are designated on a list, or the entire village will be destroyed. Portillo's name was on the roster, and rather than suffer Christian martyrdom to save his parishioners, the frightened cleric fled. And all of the remaining villagers were slaughtered. Convinced that he failed this excruciating moral test, Portillo wanders the lawless countryside, a self-proclaimed *fantasma*, a ghost condemned to find no rest. Yet a parting act of self-sacrifice, to save the lives of Fuentes and the rest of the ad hoc family that accumulates in his Jeep, finally redeems this good but troubled man.

The final traveler to join the Fuentes group is Graciela (Tania Cruz), a young peasant woman who has been suffering stomach pains and has been mute for the two years since she was raped. Her rejection of all speech is the converse of Sayles's embrace of every language. When Graciela despairs of ever finding a tranquil space beyond the brutal world in which they move, Fuentes employs the Spanish words that the author has provided to talk her out of suicide.

Two other travelers must be mentioned, though they provide the screenplay's comic relief and its weakest touches. Periodically, Fuentes crosses paths with Andrew (Mandy Patinkin) and Harriet (Kathryn Grody), two North American tourists who are crass caricatures of gringo arrogance and obtuseness. Barely bilingual, they speak Spanish, when they do, haltingly, defectively, in an accent as thick as a New York salami. "What's the word for fajitas?" asks Andrew, the burlesque of a monolingual monoculturalist who serves—in a crude, self-congratulatory way—to highlight Sayles's own accomplishment in stepping outside the *norteamericano* prison house of his native language. By contrast, the peasants who speak only Nahuatl or only Tzotzil are sentimentalized, not lampooned.

Fuentes maintains his dignity, though he speaks none of the Indian languages, and his command of English seems at least as feeble as Andrew's is of Spanish. Andrew invades Fuentes's country armed with a guide book and supreme self-confidence. Touring some ancient, pre-Columbian ruins, Andrew lectures to the doctor on the latter's own local history, and both are oblivious to present realities. The gringo derives prurient thrills from details of ancient savagery, and he presses Fuentes about whether atrocities still occur. "No aqui," replies the doctor, who insists that they occur in other countries but not in his own. Apparently immune to anything more violent than having their tires stolen, Andrew and Harriet move through the landscape as if it were an archaeological theme park. They believe that they have managed to domesticate the foreign.

However, Fuentes, like the North American viewer, is transformed by an encounter with otherness. In one of several black-and-white flashbacks that depict the training sessions the veteran physician conducted to prepare his students for service in the countryside, Fuentes reminds them that the medical project is fighting not only malignant microbes but also ignorance: "nobody is immune to this disease," he declares. *Hombres Armados* is largely the story of how Fuentes himself overcomes infection, in a film itself designed to inoculate viewers against the pestilence of ignorance. The impetus to write the screenplay came in part, claimed Sayles, from a poll during the Gulf War revealing that 60 percent of Americans did not want to know more about what was happening: "I started thinking about the phenomenon of willful ignorance," explained the author, for whom translingualism is willful awareness. "What's the cost of it? Why do people try to be ignorant of things? What happens to a person who thinks he's done something really wonderful when it turns out to be really terrible?" (Interview).

Reversing the trajectory from countryside to city that defines Gregory Nava's *El Norte* (1983), Fuentes departs the capital to vacation in the mountains. But what he discovers in the hinterlands shatters his urbane illusions about reason and progress. "Maybe innocence is a sin," observes Padre Portillo, a jaded sage defiled by harsh experience. Beside bounteous vegetation, Fuentes encounters a baby suffering from malnutrition, subsisting on coffee because market forces do not allow the crop to yield sufficient cash to support a balanced diet. He wanders through a field littered with human skulls, victims of a violence that seems devoid of rationale. Caught between the army and the rebels, civilians are tortured and murdered by each side on suspicion of supporting the other. The peasants, Padre Portillo reports, try to stay outside politics, but outside politics willy nilly intrudes into their lives. Sayles seems less sympathetic to the government, controlled by a white oligarchy for the exploitation of Indians, than the outnumbered and ill-equipped insurgents. But the film invokes a pox on both their houses for the way they have blighted people's houses throughout the countryside. One by one, Fuentes learns that none of his students, dedicated to sustaining life among the poorest of the peasants, has survived the lethal forces that are loose in the land. Arms and the man, sang Virgil, and so does Sayles, but *Hombres armados* is a dismal elegy. It is not an ode to the NRA.

When Fuentes denies that massacres are being committed in his country, the tourist Harriet replies that newspapers in the United States have reported otherwise. But Fuentes rejects such lurid journalism as untrustworthy, a device to titillate an unsophisticated public. "Newspapers are businesses, and the common people love drama," he explains, and in his dismissal he echoes the patronizing way the general has belittled rumors of military atrocities against civilians in the mountains. Fuentes and the army officer—who, like the social structure, is afflicted with a cancer that he tries to keep concealed—caution skepticism toward histrionics. Nevertheless the viewer of *Hombres Armados* learns the painful truths that drama can convey. Padre Portillo explains that he used theatrical techniques to bring the Word of God to the impressionable villagers of his ministry, and it is not too farfetched to see in that example a reflexive reference to Sayles's own cinematic art. It is through the staged make-believe of *Hombres Armados* that Sayles intends to open our innocent eyes to the continuing reality of spectacular brutality. Toward the end of the film, in Modelo, a refugee camp administered by the army, we catch a glimpse of fugitives from violence clustered around a TV set, mesmerized by electronic images of violence: men with guns shooting at other men with guns. Sayles offers an alternative to the popular celluloid dramas that anesthetize their audiences to the outrages that continue just beyond the screen.

Yet even if the common people love drama, it was unlikely that many of them would rush to see Sayles's film. In fact, *Hombres Armados* grossed less than four million dollars domestically, when a hundred million is the criterion for a Hollywood hit. Argentine actor Luppi (*Cronos, A Place in the World*) does a splendid job of capturing the dignity, benevolence, and innocence of Dr. Humberto Fuentes, but he is not a bankable star. The conventional wisdom in Hollywood is that Americans do not go to movie theaters in order to read, which is why movies about World War II tend to show the German high command barking out their orders in heavily accented English. As director and star, Kevin Costner managed to draw mass audiences and several Oscars when *Dances with Wolves* (1990) spoke Lakota Sioux. However, audiences in this country reject all but a few subtitled movies. One exception, *Like Water for Chocolate* (1993), a Mexican film directed by Alfonso Arau, proved so prosperous that it offered some false hope to those producing other films in Spanish and other films with subtitles.

Hombres Armados might be expected to appeal to the large, newly assertive Latino population of the United States and to audiences throughout the rest of the hemisphere, but for the fact that, unlike Arau's film, it lacks sex and even lacks food—except for thought. In contrast to Arau's sweet piece of cinema, Sayles's sole allusion to chocolate occurs during a campfire scene in which one guerrilla asks Fuentes to enumerate all the flavors of ice cream sold at a shop in the capital, to another rustic guerrilla who has never tasted any. Sayles's new film is an unrelenting attack on innocence that makes few concessions to viewers partial to retaining that indifferent condition. *Hombres Armados* offers a graphic indictment of the kind of apathy that allowed bystanders to claim ignorance of Nazi atrocities, thereby allowing atrocity to flourish.

The ultimate destination of Fuentes and his companions is a celestial settlement called Cerca del Cielo, a utopia rumored to exist high above all roads and beyond all men with arms. Despite determined efforts, neither the soldiers nor the guerrillas have managed to find the place. Yet Fuentes promises Graciela that it does exist, that it is "A place where each day is a gift and each person is reborn." Cerca del Cielo stands as refutation to the general's self-exculpatory contention, early in the film, that the world is a savage place—except that the settlement seems to exist just a bit above the world, where Graciela can stand smiling, gazing at the sunshine, without a need for words.

In *Thinking in Pictures*, a book he published in 1987 to describe the making of *Matewan*, Sayles explains his cinematic art: "If storytelling has a positive function it's to put us in touch with other people's lives, to help us connect and draw strength or knowledge from people we'll never meet, to help us see beyond our own experience" (11). *Hombres Armados* is another stage in Sayles's continuing effort to help us see beyond, for which language is a crucial tool to accommodate alterity. Independent filmmakers, in particular, are and need to be resilient (Sayles's continuing employment as a script doctor for such miscellaneous projects as *Alligator, The Howling, The Clan of the Cave Bear,* and *Wild Thing* eases the economic burden of making the more challenging films he directs, even if *Hombres armados* cost a mere two and a half million dollars, barely one-twentieth the average of a Hollywood production). And aside from the positive virtue in negative capability, linguistic chameleons possess a tactical advantage over those anchored in a single syntax.

Yet there are limits not only to individual resourcefulness but also to artistic empathy, and after Babel no one can be polyglot enough to filter experience through each of the six thousand extant languages. For all the range in his films, supple Sayles is unlikely to be writing a screenplay soon in Gikuyu or Malayalam. Luis Buñuel, who has directed films in each of three languages—Spanish, French, and English—would seem to be the supreme master of imaginative projection. But for the Spanish surrealist, choice of language is often more a matter of circumstance than of vision. The use of Spanish in *El Angel Exterminador* (1962), the story of a dinner party that never ends, and the use of French in *Le Charme discret de la bourgeoisie* (1972), the story of a dinner party that never quite begins, probably tells us less about the texture of each film than about its sources of funding. A willful attempt to gain access to worlds alien to Anglophonia, the use of Spanish in *Hombres Armados* is much, much more telling.

EPILOGUE

Like Louis Begley, Jerzy Kosinski was born Jewish in Poland in 1933. And while Maciek of *Wartime Lies* and, presumably, Begley himself managed to talk their way, in useful tongues, through the Holocaust, Kosinski stopped speaking entirely during the wartime years he spent hiding in the countryside. He lost all language until 1947, ten years before reinventing himself in English in the United States. Kosinski's muteness is paralleled in the act of self-mutilation and self-muting that Bharati Mukherjee's widowed Jasmine performs shortly after her arrival in Florida, as the first installment in a planned suttee. In a seedy motel room, where she has just killed the ship's captain who had smuggled her into the United States and then raped her, Jasmine slices her own tongue. The painful wound soon heals, and she is able to use that tongue to start her life again, with a new language, English. As Jasmine—now living in Iowa, "a place where the language you speak is what you are" (*Jasmine* 11)—tells her story, English comes trippingly off her wounded tongue.

Muteness hardly figures in every translingual life. And at least one monolingual author, Maya Angelou, recounts in her autobiography *I Know Why the Caged Bird Sings* (1969) how she ceased speaking for a few years after being sexually abused as a child. But Angelou's muteness prefigures the jettisoning of a victim's identity and the acquisition of a powerful new voice as a proud singer, actress, activist, and poet. And by changing tongues, authors flirt with silence. In no figure is this fact more striking than Beckett, whose texts, after the initial jump from luxuriant English to austere French, become more and more terse. Each of Beckett's garrulous narrators aspires to transcend the clamor of narration, to exhaust all language, and languages, in order to attain the silence that is truth, peace, and—for those whose lives are constructed out of words—death.

Though white—the blank—seems a sign of vacancy, it is in truth a dense amalgam of every color. Silence—toward which each of Beckett's gabbers clamor and which Kosinski, severing his breath with a plastic bag, attained—might likewise be the ultimate music of the spheres, the perfect blend of babble that at last transcends the curse of Babel. Panlingualism is the consummation of the translingual impulse. "I want articulation—but articulation that says the whole world at once," announces Eva Hoffman (*Lost* 11), whose pandictic longings cannot be satisfied by fluency merely in Polish and English. Consider the spectacle of the infant who suddenly traverses the threshold of speech: from mum to magpie. Once we begin to say anything, we yearn to say everything.

The consequences of dispersing the human species among thousands of languages with distinct phonologies, lexicons, and morphologies are not merely social—bonding us, as they do, in separate speech communities that are mutually incomprehensible and often hostile. But the legacy of the multiplicity of languages is the realization that each of us is incomplete. The limits of my language remind me of the limits of my mind. Omnitranslingualism is the impossible alternative to recovering the primal, perfect tongue, the Ur-lingua that subsumes all disparate speech, in which no thought will ever leave one at a loss for words.

In order to ascertain priorities, polyglots are often asked which language they dream in, as if dreams were some sort of linguistic polygraph registering the genuine syntax of the soul. Of course, it is perfectly possible to dream macaronically, feverishly switching codes while tossing and turning all night in bed. Or to dream in seven different languages on seven successive nights, perhaps portending, as in Pharaonic prophecy, seven fat years for professional interpreters. But if, *pace* Sigmund Freud and Delmore Schwartz, responsibilities begin in dreams, perhaps so too does the truth that lurks beyond words. Many translingual authors offer intimations of what is beyond not just the languages they know but beyond any language that they could ever know. Asked whether English, French, or Russian was the primary vehicle of his thoughts, Nabokov, as noted earlier, replied: "I don't think in any language. I think in images. I don't believe that people think in languages" (*Strong Opinions* 14). Nabokov fills his fictions with characters who, like John Shade in *Pale Fire* or the narrator of "The Vane Sisters," seek communication with voices—the ghosts of Shade's daughter, Hazel, and Cynthia Vane, respectively—that remain forever beyond their reach. Though Shade is an accomplished poet and the narrator of "The Vane Sisters" is a professor of French, their verbal prowess is woefully inadequate to the task.

"All translations aspire to pure language," Walter Benjamin declared; "For the great motif of integrating many tongues into one true language is at work" (77). Translation is a function of translingualism, which in general shares that futile aspiration. The project of traversing many tongues, of expanding one's awareness asymptotically toward universal comprehension, is doomed to imperfection. As Wittgenstein avowed in German, the language he wrote in before he switched to English, "Wovon man nicht sprechen kann, darüber muss man schweigen" [Whereof one cannot speak, thereof one must be silent (188–89)]. And that is all that can be said about that.

A ROSTER OF TRANSLINGUAL AUTHORS

Walter Abish
Chinua Achebe
Tamas Aczel
S. Y. Agnon
Ama Ata Aidoo
Chingiz Aitmatov
Vassilis Alexakis
Felipe Alfau
Alurista
Julia Alvarez
Yehuda Amichai
Alexandre Amprimoz
Mulk Raj Anand
Mary Antin
Gloria Anzaldúa
Guillaume Apollinaire
Aharon Appelfeld
Apuleius
Michael Arlen
A. K. Armah
Hans Arp
Fernando Arrabal
Isaac Asimov
Augustine
Rosa Auslander
Ausonius
Kofi Awoonor
Samuel Beckett
William Beckford
Louis Begley
Tahar Ben Jelloun
Chaim Nachman Bialik

Hector Bianciotti
Sven Birkerts
Rachid Boudgedra
Yosef Haim Brenner
Breyten Breytenbach
André Brink
Joseph Brodsky
Carlos Bulosan
Abraham Cahan
John Calvin
Elias Canetti
Giacomo Casanova
Rosalia de Castro
Catherine the Great
Paul Celan
Adelbert von Chamisso
Andrée Chedid
Louis Chu
E. M. Cioran
Zehra Cirak
Sandra Cisneros
Ernest Claes
André Codrescu
J. M. Coetzee
Joseph Conrad
Dante
Edwidge Danticat
Amma Darko
Kamala Das
René Descartes
Anita Desai
Junot Diaz

Isak Dinesen
Ariel Dorfman
Buchi Emecheta
Quintus Ennius
Erasmus
Margiad Evans
Nuruddin Farah
Farid
Raymond Federman
Rosario Ferré
Eva Figes
Teofilio Folengo
Gilbert Freire
Athol Fugard
Mehmed bin Süleyman
 Fuzulî
Romain Gary
Stefan George
Alberto Gerchunoff
William Gerhardi
Mizra Asadullah Khan
 Ghalib
Michel de Ghelderode
Khalil Gibran
Janusz Glowacki
Uri Nissan Gnessin
Nikolai Gogol
Carlo Goldoni
Yvan Goll
Jacob Gordin
Julien Green
Uri Zvi Greenberg

Fredrick Philip Grove	Rene Marqués	Luc Sante
Lars Gustafsson	Daphne Marlatt	Ken Saro-Wiwa
Yehuda Halevi	Martial	Nathalie Sarraute
Jan de Hartog	Ved Mehta	John Sayles
Ursula Hegi	Francisco Manuel	Charles Sealsfield
José-Maria de Heredia	de Melo	Ousmane Sembene
Stefan Heym	Mendele Mokher Sforim	Jorge Semprun
Hildegard of Bingen	Stuart Merrill	Seneca
Rolando Hinojosa-Smith	C. F. Meyer	Léopold Senghor
Eva Hoffman	John Milton	Vikram Seth
Vicente Huidobro	Libuse Monikova	Anton Shammas
Abraham Ibn Ezra	Thomas More	Taras Shevchenko
Solomon Ibn Gabirol	Jean Moréas	Wole Soyinka
Eugène Ionesco	Oswald Mbuyiseni	Baruch Spinoza
Muhammad Iqbal	Mtshali	Ilan Stavans
Kazuo Ishiguro	Bharati Mukherjee	George Steiner
Fazil Iskander	Charles Mungoshi	Tom Stoppard
Panait Istrati	R. K. Narayan	August Strindberg
Ruth Prawer Jhabvala	Narayanatirtha	Antonio Tabucchi
Ha Jin	Ngugi wa Thiong'o	Shaul Tchernichowsky
F. Sionil José	Anaïs Nin	Terence
Kaka Kalelkar	Jan Novak	B. Traven
Smaro Kamboureli	Flann O'Brien	Elsa Triolet
Kateb Yacine	Gabriel Okara	Henri Troyat
Jack Kerouac	Ben Okri	Gabre-Medhin Tsegaye
Abdelkébir Khatibi	Okot p'Bitek	Niccolò Tucci
Maxine Hong Kingston	Gustavo Pérez-Firmat	Ivan Turgenev
Arthur Koestler	Fernando Pessoa	Joseph Tusiani
Jerzy Kosinski	Petrarch	Fydor Ivanovich Tyutchev
Henry Kreisel	Sol T. Plaatje	Tristan Tzara
Ksettraya	Plautus	Giuseppe Ungaretti
Milan Kundera	Marco Polo	Luigi Ventura
Ewa Kuryluk	Elena Poniatowska	Francis Viélé-Griffin
Jeannette Lander	Gabriel Preil	Renée Vivien
Chin Yang Lee	Prem Chand	David Vogel
Jakov Lind	Stanislaw Przybyszewski	Phyllis Wheatley
Lin Yu-t'ang	Manuel Puig	Elie Wiesel
Clarice Lispector	Quintilian	Oscar Wilde
Lucan	Ayn Rand	R. R. Williams
Amin Maalouf	Raja Rao	Louis Wolfson
Hugh MacDairmid	Rainer Maria Rilke	Anzia Yezierska
Andreï Makine	Richard Rodriguez	Louis Zukofsky
Eduardo Manet	Salman Rushdie	
Alberto Manguel	Rafael Sabatini	
Joyce Mansour	Sa`di	
Eugene Marais	Sa'ib of Tabriz	

WORKS CITED

Achebe, Chinua. "An Image of Africa." *Massachusetts Review* 18 (1977): 782–94.
———. *Morning Yet on Creation Day*. London: Heinemann, 1975.
———. *Things Fall Apart*. Portsmouth NH: Heinemann Educational, 1996.
Alfau, Felipe. "Anonymity: An Interview with Felipe Alfau." Interview by Ilan Stavans. *Review of Contemporary Fiction* 13.1 (1993): 146–53.
———. *Chromos*. Elmwood Park IL: Dalkey Archive, 1990.
———. *Locos: A Comedy of Gestures*. Elmwood Park IL: Dalkey Archive, 1988.
———. *Sentimental Songs / La poesía cursi*. Translated by Ilan Stavans. Elmwood Park IL: Dalkey Archive, 1992.
Alvarez, Julia. *How the García Girls Lost Their Accents*. Chapel Hill NC: Algonquin, 1991.
———. *Something to Declare*. Chapel Hill NC: Algonquin, 1998.
Angelou, Maya. *I Know Why the Caged Bird Sings*. New York: Random House, 1969.
Antin, Mary. *From Plotzk to Boston*. Upper Saddle River NJ: Literature House, 1970.
———. *The Promised Land*. Edited by Werner Sollors. New York: Penguin, 1997.
———. *They Who Knock at Our Gates: A Complete Gospel of Immigration*. Boston: Houghton Mifflin, 1914.
Anzaldúa, Gloria. *Borderlands / La Frontera: The New Mestiza*. San Francisco: Aunt Lute, 1987.
Apuleius. *The Golden Ass: Being the Metamorphoses of Lucius Apuleius, with an English Translation by W. Adlington*. Loeb Classical Library. Cambridge MA: Harvard University Press, 1977.
Ascham, Roger. *English Works: Toxophilus, Report of the Affaires and State of Germany, The Scholemaster*. Edited by William Aldis Wright. New York: Cambridge University Press, 1970.
Auden, W. H. *The Dyer's Hand*. New York: Random House, 1962.
Ba`al-Makhshoves. "One Literature in Two Languages." In *What Is Jewish Literature?*, edited by Hana Wirth-Nesher, 69–77. Philadelphia: Jewish Publication Society, 1994.
Barthes, Roland. *Le Degré zéro de l'écriture*. Paris: Editions du Seuil, 1953.
Bayley, John. "English as a Second Language." *New York Times Book Review*, 1 September 1996, 6.
Beaujour, Elizabeth Klosty. *Alien Tongues: Bilingual Russian Writers of the "First" Emigration*. New York: Cornell University Press, 1989.
Beckett, Samuel. "Dante . . . Bruno. Vico . . Joyce." In *Our Exagmination round His*

    Factification for Incamination of Work in Progress, 1–22. London: Faber & Faber, 1938.

———. *Molloy*. Paris: Minuit, 1951.

———. *Three Novels: Molloy, Malone Dies, The Unnamable*. Translated by Patrick Bowles. New York: Grove, 1965.

Begley, Louis. *About Schmidt*. New York: Alfred A. Knopf, 1996.

———. *As Max Saw It*. New York: Alfred A. Knopf, 1994.

———. *The Man Who Was Late*. New York: Alfred A. Knopf, 1992.

———. *Mistler's Exit*. New York: Alfred A. Knopf, 1998.

———. *Wartime Lies*. New York: Alfred A. Knopf, 1991.

Benjamin, Walter. "The Task of the Translator." In *Illuminations*, translated by Harry Zohn, edited by Hannah Arendt, 69–82. New York: Schocken, 1969.

Birkerts, Sven. *The Gutenberg Elegies: The Fate of Reading in an Electronic Age*. New York: Fawcett Columbine, 1994.

Blanchot, Maurice. *L'Arrêt de mort*. Paris: Gallimard, 1948.

———. *Death Sentence*. Translated by Lydia Davis. Barrytown NY: Station Hill, 1978.

Borges, Jorge Luis. "Tlön, Uqbar, Orbis Tertius." Translated by Alastair Reid. In *Ficciones*, edited by Anthony Kerrigan, 17–35. New York: Grove, 1962.

Boswell, James. *Life of Johnson*. London: Oxford University Press, 1953.

Breytenbach, Breyten. *End Papers: Essays, Letters, Articles of Faith, Workbook Notes*. Boston: Faber & Faber, 1986.

———. *Return to Paradise*. Cape Town: David Philip, 1993.

Brink, André. "South African Writers and the Problem of Languages." *Commonwealth Essays and Studies* 16 (1993): 96–103.

Canetti, Elias. *Die gerettete Zunge: Geschichte einer Jugend*. Munich: Carl Hanser, 1977.

———. *The Memoirs of Elias Canetti*. Translated by Joachim Neugroschel and Ralph Manheim. New York: Farrar, Straus & Giroux, 1999.

Casanova, Giacomo. *History of My Life*. Translated by Willard R. Trask. New York: Harcourt, Brace & World, 1966.

———. *Mémoires, Tome I (1725–1744)*. Paris: Gallimard, 1967.

Chalfen, Israel. *Paul Celan: A Biography of His Youth*. Translated by Maximilian Bleyleben. New York: Persea, 1991.

Clifford, James. *Routes: Travel and Translation in the Late Twentieth Century*. Cambridge MA: Harvard University Press, 1997.

Coetzee, J. M. *Age of Iron*. New York: Random House, 1990.

———. *Boyhood: Scenes from Provincial Life*. New York: Viking Penguin, 1997.

———. *Doubling the Point: Essays and Interviews*. Edited by David Attwell. Cambridge MA: Harvard University Press, 1992.

———. *Dusklands*. New York: Penguin, 1985.

———. "The English Fiction of Samuel Beckett: An Essay in Stylistic Analysis." Ph.D. diss., University of Texas at Austin, 1969.

———. *Foe*. New York: Penguin, 1987.

———. "Homage." *Threepenny Review* 53 (1993): 5–7.

———. "An Interview with J. M. Coetzee." Interview by Jean Sévry. *Commonwealth Essays and Studies* 9 (1986): 1–7.
———. *In the Heart of the Country*. New York: Penguin, 1982.
———. *Life & Times of Michael K*. New York: Penguin, 1985.
———. *The Master of Petersburg*. New York: Viking, 1994.
———. *Waiting for the Barbarians*. New York: Penguin, 1982.
———. *White Writing: On the Culture of Letters in South Africa*. New Haven: Yale University Press, 1988.
Colmer, Rosemary. "Nuruddin Farah." In *International Literature in English: Essays on the Major Writers*, edited by Robert L. Ross, 131–42. New York: Garland, 1991.
Conrad, Joseph. Letter to Edward Garnett, 28 August 1908. In *Joseph Conrad: Life and Letters*, edited by C. Jean Aubry, 2:82–83. New York: Doubleday, Page, 1927.
———. *A Personal Record: Some Reminiscences*. Garden City NY: Doubleday, Page, 1927.
———. *The Secret Agent: A Simple Tale*. New York: Penguin, 1986.
Curtius, Ernst Robert. *Essays on European Literature: Kritische Essays zur europäischen Literatur*. Translated by Michael Kowal. Princeton: Princeton University Press, 1973.
———. *Kritische Essays zur europäischen Literatur*. Bern: A. Francke, 1950.
De Courtivron, Isabelle. "Found in Translation." *New York Times Book Review*, 20 December 1998, 31.
Deleuze, Gilles, and Félix Guattari. *Kafka: Toward a Minor Literature*. Translated by Dana Polan. Minneapolis: University of Minnesota Press, 1986.
Dorfman, Ariel. *Heading South, Looking North: A Bilingual Journey*. New York: Farrar, Straus & Giroux, 1998.
Eco, Umberto. *The Name of the Rose*. Translated by William Weaver. New York: Harcourt Brace Jovanovich, 1983.
Eliot, T. S. Interview by Donald Hall. In *Writers at Work: The "Paris Review" Interviews*, edited by George Plimpton. 2d ser., 89–110. New York: Penguin, 1963.
Ellmann, Richard. *Oscar Wilde*. New York: Alfred A. Knopf, 1988.
Emecheta, Buchi. *The Joys of Motherhood*. New York: George Braziller, 1980.
Fanon, Frantz. *Black Skin, White Masks*. Translated by Charles Lam Markmann. New York: Grove, 1967.
Federman, Raymond. *Double or Nothing*. Chicago: Swallow, 1971.
———. *Journey into Chaos: Samuel Beckett's Early Fiction*. Berkeley: University of California Press, 1965.
———. *Take It or Leave It*. New York: Fiction Collective, 1976.
———. *To Whom It May Concern*. Boulder CO: Fiction Collective Two, 1990.
———. *The Voice in the Closet / La Voix dans le cabinet*. Madison WI: Coda, 1979.
Ferré, Rosario. "Writers and Artists Speaking on the Frontier." *Review: Latin American Literature and Arts* 54 (spring 1997): 62.
Field, Andrew. *Nabokov: His Life in Part*. New York: Viking, 1977.

Forster, Leonard. *The Poet's Tongues: Multilingualism in Literature*. London: Cambridge University Press, 1970.

Gafaiti, Hafid. *Boudjedra ou la passion de la modernité*. Paris: Denoël, 1987.

Gallagher, Susan VanZanten. *A Story of South Africa: J. M. Coetzee's Fiction in Context*. Cambridge MA: Harvard University Press, 1991.

Gellius, Aulus. *The Attic Nights of Aulus Gellius with an English Translation by John C. Rolfe*. Vol. 3. Loeb Classical Library. Cambridge MA: Harvard University Press, 1978.

Gessner, Niklaus. *Die Unzulänglichkeit der Sprache: eine Untersuchung über Formzerfall und Beziehunglosigkeit bei Samuel Beckett*. Zurich: Juris, 1957.

Goldoni, Carlo. *Mémoires, pour servir à l'histoire de sa vie et à celle de son théâtre*. Vol. 2. Geneva: Slatkine, 1968.

———. *Memoirs of Carlo Goldoni*. Translated by John Black. Westport CT: Greenwood, 1976.

Gordimer, Nadine. "The Idea of Gardening." Review of *Life & Times of Michael K*, by J. M. Coetzee. *New York Review of Books*, 2 February 1984, 3, 6.

Grove, Frederick Philip. *A Search for America: The Odyssey of an Immigrant*. Toronto: McClelland & Stewart, 1971.

Hendrickson, Robert. *American Literary Anecdotes*. New York: Penguin, 1992.

Hinojosa-Smith, Rolando. *Mi querido Rafa*. Houston: Arte Público, 1981.

Hoffman, Eva. *Exit into History: A Journey through the New Eastern Europe*. New York: Viking, 1993.

———. "The Grotesque in Modern Fiction." Ph.D. diss., Harvard University, 1975.

———. *Lost in Translation: A Life in a New Language*. New York: Penguin, 1990.

Humboldt, Wilhelm von. *Catium and Hellas*. Translated by Marian Cowan. In *Critical Theory since Plato*, edited by Hazard Adams, 483–84. Rev. ed. Fort Worth TX: Harcourt Brace Jovanovich College Publishers, 1992.

Isola, Akinwumi. "The African Writer's Tongue." *Research in African Literatures* 23.1 (spring 1992): 17–26.

Jefferson, Thomas. Letter to John Bannister Jr., 15 October 1785. In *Writings*, 837–40. Library of America 17. New York: Literary Classics of the United States, 1984.

Johnson, D. Barton. "The Ambidextrous Universe of *Look at the Harlequins!*" In *Critical Essays on Vladimir Nabokov*, edited by Phyllis A. Roth, 202–15. Boston: G. K. Hall, 1984.

Joyce, James. *A Portrait of the Artist as a Young Man*. New York: Viking, 1956.

Kafka, Franz. "Couriers." In *The Basic Kafka*, 185. New York: Pocket Books, 1979.

Koestler, Arthur. *Bricks to Babel: A Selection from Fifty Years of His Writings, Chosen and with New Commentary by the Author*. New York: Random House, 1981.

Krige, Uys. *Orphan of the Desert*. Cape Town: John Malherbe, 1967.

Krueger, John R. "Nabokov's Zemblan: A Constructed Language of Fiction." *Linguistics* 31 (1967): 44–49.

Lerner, Gerda. *Why History Matters: Life and Thought*. New York: Oxford University Press, 1997.

MacShane, Frank. *The Life and Work of Ford Madox Ford.* New York: Horizon, 1965.
Mann, Thomas. *Der Zauberberg.* Berlin: S. Fischer, 1974.
Matisse, Henri. *Jazz.* Munich: Piper, 1957.
Mazrui, Ali A. *The Political Sociology of the English Language: An African Perspective.* The Hague: Mouton, 1975.
Megroz, R. L. *Joseph Conrad's Mind and Method: A Study of Personality in Art.* New York: Russell & Russell, 1964.
Meyer, Priscilla. *Find What the Sailor Has Hidden: Vladimir Nabokov's "Pale Fire."* Middletown CT: Wesleyan University Press, 1988.
Miller, Jane. "Writing in a Second Language." *Raritan* 2 (1982): 115–32.
Miron, Dan. *A Traveler Disguised: A Study in the Rise of Modern Yiddish.* New York: Schocken, 1973.
Mukherjee, Bharati. *Jasmine.* New York: Grove Weidenfeld, 1989.
Nabokov, Vladimir. *The Annotated Lolita.* Edited by Alfred Appel Jr. New York: McGraw-Hill, 1970.
———. *Look at the Harlequins!.* New York: Vintage International, 1990.
———. *The Nabokov-Wilson Letters: Correspondence between Vladimir Nabokov and Edmund Wilson 1940–1971.* Edited by Simon Karlinsky. New York: Harper & Row, 1979.
———. "On a Book Entitled *Lolita*." In *The Annotated Lolita*, edited by Alfred Appel Jr., 318–19. New York: McGraw-Hill, 1970.
———. *Pale Fire.* New York: Vintage International, 1989.
———. *Pnin.* New York: Vintage International, 1989.
———. *Speak, Memory: An Autobiography Revisited.* New York: G. P. Putnam's Sons, 1966.
———. *The Stories of Vladimir Nabokov.* New York: Alfred A. Knopf, 1995.
———. *Strong Opinions.* New York: McGraw-Hill, 1973.
Ndebele, Njabulo. Interview by Jane Wilkinson. In *Talking with African Writers: Interviews with African Poets, Playwrights and Novelists*, edited by Jane Wilkinson, 147–57. Portsmouth NH: Heinemann, 1992.
Ngugi wa Thiong'o. *Decolonising the Mind: The Politics of Language in African Literature.* Portsmouth NH: Heinemann, 1986.
———. Interview by Aminu Abdullahi. In *African Writers Talking: A Collection of Radio Interviews*, edited by Cosmo Pieterse and Dennis Duerden, 124–31. New York: Africana, 1972.
———. *Moving the Centre: The Struggle for Cultural Freedoms.* Portsmouth NH: Heinemann, 1993.
Niger, Shmuel. *Bilingualism in the History of Jewish Literature.* Translated by Joshua A. Fogel. New York: University Press of America, 1990.
Okara, Gabriel. "African Speech . . . English Words." In *African Writers on African Writing*, edited by G. D. Killam, 137–39. Evanston IL: Northwestern University Press, 1973.
Okrand, Marc. *The Klingon Dictionary: English-Klingon, Klingon-English.* New York: Pocket Books, 1995.
Pérez Firmat, Gustavo. *Bilingual Blues: Poems, 1981–1994.* Tempe AZ: Bilingual Press, 1995.

Pessoa, Fernando. *Always Astonished: Selected Prose*. Edited and translated by Edwin Honig. San Francisco: City Lights, 1988.

Plante, David. *The Accident*. New York: Ticknor & Fields, 1991.

Puig, Manuel. *Eternal Curse on the Reader of These Pages*. New York: Random House, 1982.

Rilke, Rainer Maria. *Rilke und Russland: Briefe, Erinnerungen, Gedichte*. Edited by Konstantin Asadowski. Berlin: Aufbau-Verlag, 1986.

Rao, Raja. *Kanthapura*. Westport CT: Greenwood, 1977.

———. "Raja Rao." In *Interviews with Writers of the Post-Colonial World*, edited by Feroza Jussawalla and Reed Way Dasenbrock, 140–55. Jackson: University Press of Mississippi, 1992.

Said, Edward W. *Culture and Imperialism*. New York: Alfred A. Knopf, 1993.

Santayana, George. *Poems*. New York: Charles Scribner's Sons, 1923.

Sante, Luc. *The Factory of Facts*. New York: Pantheon, 1998.

Sapir, Edward. "The Status of Linguistics as a Science." *Language* 5 (1929): 207–14.

Sayles, John. *Los Gusanos*. New York: HarperCollins, 1991.

———. *Hombres Armados / Men with Guns*. Sony Pictures, 1997. Film.

———. Interview by author. 11 December 1997.

———. *Thinking in Pictures: The Making of the Movie "Matewan."* Boston: Houghton Mifflin, 1987.

Senghor, Léopold. "Le Français, Langue de culture." *Esprit* 30 (1962): 837–44.

Shakespeare, William. *Timon of Athens*. In *The Complete Works of Shakespeare*, edited by Hardin Craig, 1017–43. Chicago: Scott, Foresman, 1961.

Shammas, Anton. *Arabesques*. Translated by Vivian Eden. New York: Harper & Row, 1988.

———. "My Case Is Hopeless." Interview by Anne Zusy. *New York Times Book Review*, 17 April 1988, 48.

Shaw, George Bernard. "Maxims for Revolutionists." In *Complete Plays, with Prefaces* 3:729–43. New York: Dodd, Mead, 1962.

Shklovsky, Victor. "Art as Technique." Translated by Lee T. Lemon and Marion J. Reis. In *Critical Theory since Plato*, edited by Hazard Adams, 750–59. Rev. ed. Orlando FL: Harcourt Brace Jovanovich, 1992.

Sollors, Werner, ed. *Multilingual America: Transnationalism, Ethnicity, American Literature*. New York: New York University Press, 1998.

Soyinka, Wole. "Ethics, Ideology and the Critic." In *Criticism and Ideology: Second African Writers' Conference, Stockholm, 1986*, edited by Kirsten Holst Petersen, 26–51. Uppsala: Scandinavian Institute of African Studies, 1988.

Spencer, John, ed. *Language in Africa*. Cambridge: Cambridge University Press, 1963.

Spettigue, Douglas O. *FPG: The European Years*. Ottawa: Oberon, 1973.

Stavans, Ilan. *Art and Anger: Essays on Politics and the Imagination*. Albuquerque: University of New Mexico Press, 1996.

Steiner, George. *After Babel*. New York: Oxford University Press, 1975.

———. *Extraterritorial: Papers on Literature and the Language Revolution*. New York: Atheneum, 1971.

Stokes, Geoffrey, and Eliot Fremont-Smith. "Jerzy Kosinski's Tainted Words." *Village Voice*, 22 June 1982, 1, 41–43.

Thurman, Judith. *Isak Dinesen: The Life of Karen Blixen*. London: Weidenfeld & Nicholson, 1982.

Tusiani, Joseph. *Gente Mia*. Stone Park IL: Italian Cultural Center, 1978.

Wagner, Richard. "Jews in Music." In *Wagner on Music and Drama: A Compendium of Richard Wagner's Prose Works*, edited by Albert Goldman and Evert Sprinchorn, translated by H. Ashton Ellis, 51–59. New York: E. P. Dutton, 1964.

Wali, Obiajunwa. "The Dead End of African Literature." *Transition* 10 (1963): 13–15.

Whorf, Benjamin Lee. *Language, Thought, and Reality: Selected Writings*. Edited by John B. Carroll. Cambridge MA: MIT Press, 1956.

Wilde, Oscar. "The Censure and *Salomé*." Interview by Robert Ross. In *Oscar Wilde: Interviews and Recollections*, edited by E. H. Mikhail, 1:186–89. New York: Barnes & Noble, 1979. Originally published in *Pall Mall Budget*, 30 June 1892.

Willemse, Hein. "The Black Afrikaans Writer: A Continuing Dichotomy." In *From South Africa: New Writing, Photographs, and Art*, edited by David Bunn and Jane Taylor, 236–46. Chicago: University of Chicago Press, 1988.

Wittgenstein, Ludwig. *Tractatus Logico-Philosophicus*. Edited and translated by C. K. Ogden. Boston: Routledge & Kegan Paul, 1981.

Wolfson, Louis. *Le Schizo et les langues*. Paris: Gallimard, 1971.

Wyclif, John. *Select English Works of John Wyclif*. Edited by Thomas Arnold. Vol. 3. Oxford: Clarendon, 1871.

Yeats, William Butler. Letter to William Rothenstein, 7 May 1935. In *The Letters of W. B. Yeats*, edited by Allan Wade, 834–35. New York: Octagon, 1980.

Zabus, Chantal. *The African Palimpsest: Indigenization of Language in the West African Europhone Novel*. Atlanta: Rodopi, 1991.

INDEX

Achad Ha-Am (Asher Ginzberg), 88
Achebe, Chinua, ix, 25, 38, 40, 42, 46, 103; *Things Fall Apart,* 46
Adamov, Arthur, 7
Adams, Henry, 76
Adorno, Theodor, 83
African language debate, 44–47
African translingualism, 38–49
Afrikaans, 25, 43, 44, 47–48, 51
Agnon, S. Y. (Shmuel Yosef Czaczkes), 7, 21, 42, 88, 103
Aidoo, Ama Ata, 40
Aitmatov, Chingiz, 12
Alfau, Felipe, 27, 32, 103; *Chromos,* 29–30
Alexakis, Vassilis, 12, 33
Alvarez, Julia: *How the García Girls Lost Their Accents,* 10; *Something to Declare,* 14, 103
Amali, Samson O. O., 47
ambilingual translingualism, 12–14, 41–42, 63–64
Amichai, Yehuda, 17
Angelou, Maya: *I Know Why the Caged Bird Sings,* 113
Antin, Mary (Mashinke), ix, 73–85; *From Plotzk to Boston,* 73; *The Promised Land,* 73–85; *They Who Knock at Our Gates,* 75
Antin, Pinchus (Mary Antin's father), 79

Antonioni, Michelangelo: *Zabriskie Point,* 103
Anzaldúa, Gloria, 34–35, 42; *Borderlands/La Frontera,* 15
Apollinaire, Guillaume, 17
Apuleius, 8, 10, 39; *The Golden Ass,* 8–9
Arau, Alfonso, 103; *Like Water for Chocolate,* 111
Arlen, Michael, 14
Armah, A. K., 40
Arp, Hans (Jean), 31
Arrabal, Fernando, 7, 45
Arte Público Press: Recovery project, xi
artificial languages, vii
Ascham, Roger, 9
Asimov, Isaac, 14
Attwell, David, 51
Auden, W. H., 5–6, 43
Augustine, 8, 39, 51
Aulus Gellius, 9
Ausonius, 8
Austen, Jane, 99
Awoonor, Kofi, 45

Ba'al-Makhshoves (Isidor Eliashev), 86, 87
Babel, vii, 49, 82
Balmont, Konstantin: Russian translation of "The Bells," 68–69
Bancroft, Anne, 102
Barth, John, 4

Barthes, Roland, 64
Basçillar, Seyfettin, 6
Basque, 42
Baudelaire, Charles, 13
Bayley, John, 11
Beaujour, Elizabeth Klosty: *Alien Tongues*, xi, 33–34
Beckett, Samuel, ix, x, 7, 12, 28, 30, 33, 35, 38, 51, 52–56, 60, 62, 63, 69, 77, 103, 113–14; *Molloy*, 58–59; *Waiting for Godot*, 56; *Watt*, 53
Beethoven, Ludwig von, 13
Begley, Louis, 88–101, 113 ; *About Schmidt*, 97–99, 101; *As Max Saw It*, 92–97, 101; *The Man Who Was Late*, 90–92, 101; *Mistler's Exit*, 89, 99–101; *Wartime Lies*, 89–90, 100, 101, 113
Bellay, Joachim du, 42
Bellow, Saul, 84
Benny, Jack, 102
Bergman, Ingmar: *The Touch*, 103
Bialik, Chaim Nachman, 42, 88
Bierstadt, Albert, 5
Birkerts, Sven, 34
Blake, William, 1
Blanchot, Maurice: *L'Arrêt de Mort*, 26–27
Borges, Jorge Luis, 66, 77
Boswell, James, 11
Boudgedra, Rachid, 40, 42, 46
Bowles, Paul, 1, 6
Brenner, Yosef Chaim, 88
Breytenbach, Breyten, 25, 40, 47–49
Brink, André, 12, 33, 40, 41, 45–46, 63
Britten, Benjamin, 5
Brodsky, Joseph, 11, 63; *So Forth: Poems*, 11
Brooks, Mel, 102
Browning, Robert, 38
Buñuel, Luis: *El Angel Exterminador*, 112; *Le Charme discret de la bourgeoisie*, 112

calques, 10–11, 22
Cahan, Abraham, *Yekl*, 13
Caliban, 49

Camoens, Luis de, 41
Camus, Albert, 61; *L'Etranger*, 64
Canetti, Elias, 3, 7, 14, 24; *Die gerettete Zunge*, 21
Casanova, Giacomo, 37
Castro, Rosalia de, 12
Catherine the Great, 20
Catullus, 89
Cavafy, Constantine, 56
Celan, Paul (Paul Antschel), 3, 21, 23, 32, 103
Cervantes, Lorna Dee, 42
Cervantes, Miguel de, 18; *Don Quixote*, 196
Césaire, Aimé, 61
Chamisso, Adelbert von, 14
Chardonne, Jacques: *Demi-jour*, 100
Charles V, 13
Chaucer, Geoffrey, 42
Chedid, Andrée, 40
Choctaw, vii
Chomsky, Noam, 23, 82
Cirak, Zehra, 17
Cisneros, Sandra, 42
Claes, Ernest, 12, 45
Clifford, James, 4
Cocteau, Jean, 1
code-switching, 15–16, 42
Coetse, Jacobus, 52
Coetzee, J. M., ix, 50–62; *Age of Iron*, 55, 57, 61; *Boyhood*, 50, 57; *Dusklands*, 52, 59, 61; "The English Fiction of Samuel Beckett," 52; *Foe*, 55–56, 61; *In the Heart of the Country*, 55, 57, 61; "Homage," 54; "Isaac Newton and the Ideal of a Transparent Scientific Language," 60; *Life & Times of Michael K*, 55, 57, 61; *The Master of Petersburg*, 60, 62; "Nabokov's *Pale Fire* and the Primacy of Art," 59–60; "The Narrative of Jacobus Coetzee," 61; *Waiting for the Barbarians*, 55, 56, 61; *White Writing*, 58
Coleridge, Samuel Taylor: "The Rime of the Ancient Mariner," 78
colonialism, 42

Conrad, Jessie, 10–11
Conrad, Joseph (Jozef Teodor Konrad Korzeniowski), ix, 7, 10–11, 14, 22, 38, 51, 60, 69, 78, 103; *Heart of Darkness,* 39, 107; *Nostromo,* 99; *The Secret Agent,* 11; *Under Western Eyes,* 60
Cortázar, Julio, 6
Costner, Kevin: *Dances with Wolves,* 111
creoles, 15
Curtis, Tony, 102
Curtius, Ernst Robert, 21
Curtiz, Michael, 103

Dante Alighieri, 9, 28, 42, 43, 90
Darko, Amma, 17
Das, Kamala (Madhavikutti), 13, 20, 53, 63
defamiliarization in literature *(ostranenie),* 29–32, 41
Defoe, Daniel, *Robinson Crusoe,* 55
de Kooning, Willem, 5
Deleuze, Gilles, 49
Del Toro, Guillermo, 103
Demosthenes, 1
Denny, Neville, 39
Descartes, René, 8
Diaghilev, Sergey, 99
Díaz, Junot: *Drown,* 32
Dinesen, Isak (Karen Blixen), 2, 20, 33, 103; *Seven Gothic Tales,* 13–14, 40
Dorfman, Ariel, 103; *Heading South, Looking North,* 14–15
Dostoyevsky, Fyodor Mikhaylovich, 60–61, 62; *The Possessed,* 60
Du Bois, W. E. B., 34
du Toit, G. M., 43

Eco, Umberto: *Il Nome Della Rosa,* 18
Eichenbaum, Boris, 29
Elgar, Edward, 5
Eliot, T. S., x, 19, 54, 76, 87; *The Waste Land,* 16
Emecheta, Buchi, 2, 40; *The Joys of Motherhood,* 11
English, viii, 51, 53
Ennius, Quintus, 9

Equiano, Olaudah, 42
Erasmus, 8
Escher, M. C., 34
Esperanto, 7, 66
Evans, Margiad (Peggy Eileen Whistler), 21

Fanon, Frantz, 37
Farah, Nuruddin, 40, 45
Faulkner, William, 54
Federman, Raymond, ix, 28, 59
Ferré, Rosario, 12, 31, 103
fictional translingualism, 18–19
Figes, Eva, 17
Finnish, 42
Fitzgerald, F. Scott, 88; *The Great Gatsby,* 90
Flaubert, Gustave, 11
Ford, Ford Madox, 51; *The Good Soldier,* 51, 97
Forster, Leonard: *The Poet's Tongues,* xi
Franklin, Benjamin, viii
Fremont-Smith, Eliot, 80
French, 19–20, 25–26, 37–38, 53
Freud, Sigmund, 114
Frost, Robert, 83
Fuzulî, Mehmed bin Süleyman, 12

García Lorca, Federico, 6
Garcilaso de la Vega: *Comentarios reals,* 7
Gastarbeiterliteratur, 17
George, Stefan, 16, 21, 33, 43; *Lingua Romana,* 18
Gerhardi, William, 9–10
German, 24
Geulincx, Arnold, 28
Ghalib, Mizra Asadullah Khan, 12
Ghelderode, Michel de, 7
Gnessin, Uri Nissan, 88
Goethe, Johann Wolfgang von, 2, 87
Gogol, Nikolai, 14, 60
Goldberg, Lea, 2
Goldman, Francisco: *The Long Night of White Chickens,* 106

Goldoni, Carlo, 45; *La Bouillotte*, 19–20
Goll, Yvan, 14, 36
Goncourt, Edmond de, 19
Gombrowicz, Witold, 6, 77
Gordimer, Nadine, 61
Gordin, Jacob, 36
Gorky, Arshile, 5
Grabau, Amadeux William (husband of Mary Antin), 75
Graves, Robert, 6
Green, Julien, 13
Greenberg, Uri Zvi, 43, 88
Grove, Frederick Philip (Felix Paul Greve), 21
Guattari, Félix, 49
Gustafsson, Lars, 6

Halevi, Yehuda, 13, 87
Handel, George Frideric, 4
Hawthorne, Nathaniel, "Rappaccini's Daughter," 18
Head, Bessie, 61
Hebrew, 25, 42, 85–88
Heine, Heinrich, 87
Hemingway, Ernest, 6
Heredia, José-Maria de, 12, 17, 45
Herodotus, 4
Hildegard, Saint, of Bingen, 18
Hinojosa-Smith, Rolando: *Klail City Death Trip*, 15–16, 104
Hoffman, Eva (Ewa Wydra), ix, 4, 73–77, 80–85; *Exit into History*, 75–76; "The Grotesque in Modern Fiction," 77; *Lost in Translation*, 14, 17, 74–77, 80–84, 114
Hoffmann, Hans, 5
Hölderlin, Friedrich, 22
Homer, vii
Horace, 8
Huidobro, Vicente, 12
Humboldt, Wilhelm von, viii, 60
Hutton, Denys Finch, 40

Ibn Ezra, Abraham, 13, 87
Ibn Gabirol, Solomon, 13, 87

Idziak, Slawomir, 105
immigration, 17–18, 42
Incubus, 7
indigenization, 46–47
Ionesco, Eugène, 7, 17, 30
Iqbal, Muhammad, 12
Irish Gaelic, 42
Ishiguro, Kazuo, 14, 17
Iskander, Fazil, 14
Isola, Akinwumi, 44

Jackson, Bo, 70
James, Henry, 97, 99
Jameson, Frederic, 29
Jefferson, Thomas, ix, 87
Jewish literature, 83–88
Jhabvala, Ruth Prawer, 17
Johnson, D. Barton, 63
Johnson, Samuel, 11
Jonson, Ben, 3
Jordan, Michael, 1, 70
Joyce, James, 6, 28, 35, 38, 70; *Finnegans Wake*, 16

Kafka, Franz, 9, 49, 55, 77; "Couriers," 49
Kalelkar, Kaka, 12
Kalevala, 42
Kateb Yacine, 7, 12, 40, 44, 87
Keats, John, 33–34, 38, 40
Kennedy, John F., 10
Khatibi, Abdelkébir, 40, 47; *Amour bilingue*, 47
Kipling, Rudyard, 61
Klingon, 18, 66
Koestler, Arthur, 30–31
Kosinski, Jerzy, 79–80, 113, 114
Krige, Uys, 32, 47
Krueger, John R., 66
Ksettraya, 13
Kundera, Milan, 12, 17, 63, 76
Kunene, Mazisi, 42

la Guma, Alex, 61
Lander, Jeannette, xi, 14

Lang, Fritz, 103
Latin, 25, 42
Laye, Camara, 25
Lerner, Gerda, 4, 5
linguistic determinism, 23–24, 53, 70
Lin Yu-t'ang, 12
Lispector, Clarice, 7, 17
Livius, Andronicus, 7
Lombard, Carole, 102
Longfellow, Henry Wadsworth, 11–12, 76
Longfellow Institute, Harvard University, xi
Lowry, Malcolm, 6
Lubitsch, Ernst, 103; *To Be or Not to Be,* 102
Lucan, 8
Luppi, Federico, 110

MacDiarmid, Hugh (Christopher Murray Grieve), 21
MacNeice, Louis, 43
Macpherson, James: *Ossian,* 18
Maillu, David, 42
Makine, Andreï: *Le Testament français,* 19
Malamud, Bernard, 84
Mallarmé, Stéphane, 11
Malraux, André, 61
Mamoulian, Rouben, 103
Mandoki, Luis, 103
Manguel, Alberto, 103
Mann, Thomas, 6; *Death in Venice,* 99; *Der Zauberberg,* 27
Mansour, Joyce, 2
Marais, Eugene, 43
Martí, José, 6
Martial, 8
Mazrui, Ali, 46
Matisse, Henri: *Jazz,* 5
Melo, Francisco Manuel de, 12–13
Melville, Herman: *Moby-Dick,* 13
Mendele Mokher Sforim, 12, 33, 63, 87
Meyer, C. F., 22, 43
Meyer, Patricia, 66

Michaux, Henri, 1
Michelangelo, 1
Mikhalkov, Nikita, *Burnt by the Sun,* 106
Miller, Jane: "Writing in a Second Language," xi
Milos, Milos, 7
Miłosz, Czesław, 6
Milton, John, vii, 3
Miron, Dan, 87–88
Mishima, Yukio, 1
monolingual translingualism, 12, 14–15, 42, 63
More, Thomas, 8
Morrison, Toni, 15
mother tongue, ix
Mozart, Wolfgang Amadeus: *Don Giovanni,* 99
Mphahlele, Es'kia, 25
Mtshali, Oswald Mbuyiseni, 41
Mukařovskỳ, Jan, 29
Mukherjee, Bharati, 2; *Jasmine,* 29, 113
Mungoshi, Charles, 41

Nabokov, Dmitri, 33
Nabokov, Vladimir, ix, 2–3, 4, 7, 8, 10, 12, 33, 38, 63–72, 76, 103, 114–15; autobiographies, 69; on Beckett, 69; *Bend Sinister,* 65; on Conrad, 69; on his own English, 70; *Lolita,* 4, 13, 33, 70, 71; *Pale Fire,* 59–60, 64–72, 115; *Pnin,* 64, 65, 71; *The Real Life of Sebastian Knight,* 63; as V. Sirin, 63; "Solus Rex," 65; *Speak, Memory,* 10; "Terra Incognita," 65; translation of *Alice's Adventures in Wonderland,* 68; translation of Pushkin, 33, 68; translations of Yeats, Tennyson, Byron, Keats, Gogol, et al, 68; "The Vane Sisters," 115
Naipaul, V. S., 61
Narayan, R. K., 38, 103
Narayanatirtha, 13
Nava, Gregory: *El Norte,* 109
Ndebele, Njabulo, 43

negative capability, 33–34, 40–41
Newton, Sir Isaac, 60
Ngugi wa Thiong'o (James Ngugi), 22, 41, 43, 44, 63, 87
Niger, Shmuel, 86
Novalis (Friedrich Leopold, Baron von Hardenberg), 22

O'Brien, Flann (Brian O'Nolan and Myles na gCopaleen), 13, 20, 63
O'Connor, Flannery, 77
Odyssey, 7, 71
O. Henry (William Sydney Porter), 99
Okara, Gabriel, 40, 47; *The Voice*, 47
Okot p'Bitek, 13, 41
Okrand, Marc: *The Klingon Dictionary*, 18, 66
Omar Khayyam, 34
Oppenheimer, J. Robert, 27
Orwell, George, 61
ostranenie (defamiliarization), 29–32, 41
Ovid, 6
Owen, Wilfred, 43
Oyono-Mbia, Guillaume, 41

panlingualism, x, 48, 114–15
papal blessing, 23
Pérez-Firmat, Gustavo, "Dedication," 31–32
Pessoa, Fernando, 34, 40–41, 48, 63, 103; as Alberto Caeiro, 41; as Alvaro de Campos, 41; as Ricardo Reis, 41; as Alexander Search, 20, 41
Petrarch, 12
Plaatje, Sol T., 40
Plante, David: *The Accident*, 25–26
Poe, Edgar Allan: "The Bells," 68–69
political implications of language, 36–37
Polo, Marco, 7
Poniatowska, Elena, 14, 17
Pound, Ezra, 6, 38, 54, 99; *Cantos*, 16
Prem Chand, 12
Psamtik, 4–5
pseudonyms, 20–21

Puenzo, Luis, 103
Puig, Manuel, 103; *Eternal Curse on the Reader of These Pages*, 18
Purcell, Henry, 5
Pushkin, Alexander, 33
Pynchon, Thomas, 4

Quintilian, 8

Rachmaninoff, Sergei, 68–69
Rand, Ayn, 11
Rao, Raja, 22, 38
Reed, Ishmael, 15
Rhodes, Cecil, 46
Rilke, Rainer Maria, 2, 19, 54, 63
Rodker, John, 51
Rodriguez, Richard: *Hunger of Memory*, 14
Rölvaag, O. E., 6
Roth, Henry: *Call It Sleep*, 47
Roth, Philip, 84
Rothko, Mark, 5
Rushdie, Salman, 4, 14, 38, 61

Sabatini, Rafael, 12
Sachs, Nelly, 6
Sa'di, 13
Sa'ib of Tabriz, 13
Said, Edward: *Culture and Imperialism*, 61
Sanders, Deion, 70
Santayana, George, 2, 87
Sante, Luc: *The Factory of Facts*, 14
Sapir, Edward, 23, 24
Sapir-Whorf thesis, 36, 45, 53
Saro-Wiwa, Ken, 41
Sarraute, Nathalie, 7, 30
Sayles, John, 102–12; *The Brother from Another Planet*, 102–3; *City of Hope*, 103; *Los Gusanos*, 16, 104; *Hombres armados*, 16, 103–12; *Lianna*, 102; *Limbo*, 103; *Lone Star*, 103, 104; *Matewan*, 103; *Thinking in Pictures*, 111
Schiller, Friedrich von, 3
Schulz, Bruno, 76

Schwartz, Delmore, 114
Sealsfield, Charles (Karl Anton Post), 20
Sembene, Ousmane, 1
Seneca, 8
Senghor, Léopold, 14, 40, 42, 44, 103
Shahn, Ben, 5
Shakespeare, William, 1, 3, 34, 40; *Henry V*, 3; *The Merchant of Venice*, 98; *Timon of Athens*, 67–69
Shammas, Anton: *Arabesques*, 25
Shatner, William, 7
Shaw, George Bernard, 2
Shell, Marc, xi
Shklovsky, Victor, 29
Shlonsky, Abraham, 88
silence, 113–15
Singer, Isaac Bashevis, 6
Sirk, Douglas, 103
Smith, Red, 2
Sollors, Werner, xi
Solzhenitsyn, Alexander, 6
South Africa, 39
Soweto demonstrations, 44
Soyinka, Wole, 7, 14, 25, 39–40, 42, 61
Spanish, 103–5, 111–12
Spartacus, 102
Spettigue, D. O.: *FPG: The European Years*, 21
Spinoza, Baruch: *Ethica*, 8
Springall, Alejandro, 104
Stavans, Ilan, xii, 32, 103
Stein, Gertrude, 6
Steiner, George, 3, 7, 9
Stella, Joseph, 5
Stephansson, Stephan G., 6
Sternberg, Josef von, 103
Stevens, Leslie, 7
Stokes, Geoffrey, 80
Stoppard, Tom, 7, 14, 17
Stravinsky, Igor, 99

Tabucchi, Antonio, 13
Tagore, Rabindranath, ix–x
Tchernichowsky, Shaul, 32, 42
Teatro Campesino, 36
Tennyson, Alfred, Lord: "Ulysses," 98
Terence, 8, 39
Theater of the Absurd, 7
Thomas, Dylan, 43
Thorpe, Jim, 70
Thurman, Judith, 40
To Be or Not to Be (1942 and 1983 versions), 102
Tolkien, J. R. R., 18, 66
Tolstoy, Leo: *War and Peace*, 20
translation, 32–33
translingualism as liberation, 27–29, 36
Trilling, Lionel, 87
Triolet, Elsa, 2, 13
Tschernichowsky, Shaul, 88
Tsegaye, Gabre-Medhin, 13, 40, 41
Tsvetaeva, Marina, 2
Tusiani, Joseph, 35
Tutuola, Amos, 41
Tzara, Tristan, 14, 45

"ulogian" fiction, 65
Ungaretti, Giuseppe, 13, 32

Valdez, Luis, 36
Valéry, Paul, 22
Van Gogh, Vincent, 6
Vassalli, Sebastiano: *Narcissus*, 16
Ventura, Luigi, xi
vernaculars, 9
Vian, Boris: *J'irai cracher sur vos tombes*, 18
Virgil, 8, 89
Vivien, Renée (Pauline Tarn), 21
Voltaire: *Candide*, 18

Wagner, Richard, 86–87, 92
Wali, Obiajunwa, 43
Walpole, Horace: *The Castle of Otranto*, 18
Weber, Max, 5
Weiss, Peter, 6
Weltman, Moshe Hayyim (uncle of Mary Antin), 73
West, Nathanael, 77
Wharton, Edith, 99

Wheatley, Phyllis, 17
Whorf, Benjamin Lee, 24, 45, 47, 59, 60, 70, 82, 104
Wiesel, Elie, 7, 14
Wilde, Oscar, 63; *Salomé*, 19, 25
Wilder, Billy, 103
Willemse, Hein, 43
Williams, R. R.: *Dafydd Morgan*, 18
Wilson, Edmund, 69
Wittgenstein, Ludwig, 9, 59, 104, 115
Wolfson, Louis: *Le Schizo et les langues*, 24, 71–72
Wordsworth, William, x, 46

Wright, Richard, 49
Wyclif, John, 9

Yeats, William Butler, ix–x, 87
Yezierska, Anzia, 17
Yiddish, 87–88
Yourcenar, Marguérite, 6

Zabus, Chantal, 39, 46
Zamenhof, Ludwig Lazarus, 66, 87
Zemblan, 64–68, 71–72
Zinnemann, Fred, 103